INCREASE YOUR VOCABULARY

JOHN G. GILMARTIN

Superintendent of Schools, Waterbury, Conn.

Author of

Word Study,

Building Your Vocabulary,

Words in Action

Second Edition

Illustrations by

Lou Mortison

Cartoonist for

Waterbury *Republican-American*

PRENTICE-HALL INC.

Englewood Cliffs, N. J.

1963

Library of Congress
Catalog Card No.: 57-9793

Preface

Lack of confidence in the ability to use words exactly and effectively is no occasion for despair, because no goal is easier of attainment and no subject matter more interesting than an ample vocabulary. To attain the desired objective, the primary requisites are a real desire on the part of the student to enrich and increase his fund of words, and a resolve to adhere to a systematic plan of study.

The purpose of this book is to arouse in the student an ardent desire for word cultivation. This purpose can be realized by enabling him to see the benefits that he will derive from the possession of a masterful and practical vocabulary, and the ease with which his storehouse of words can be increased. An attempt is made to vitalize the learning of word usage by presenting various types of exercises and distributing throughout the text numerous lessons containing games or quizzes.

In addition to exercises relating to definitions and pronunciations, many will be found that pertain to *root words, spelling, multiple meanings and uses, words frequently confused, diacritical marks, adjectival usage, and figurative speech.* The words selected were not chosen from any one list, but are the result of more than a quarter of a century devoted to the teaching of vocabulary to school, college, professional, and business groups. It is safe to say that if the reader will assimilate a reasonable portion of the subject matter found in this book, he will possess a forceful and practical vocabulary that will prove most beneficial in his everyday life.

For conclusive proof that there is a real need for remedial work in the various areas of vocabulary building, the inventory tests at the beginning of the book should be worked without any special preparation. The results will furnish concrete evidence that much can be done by everyone to increase his word power.

The author wishes to express his gratitude to his wife, Irene M. Gilmartin, for her careful reading of the manuscript and the many valuable suggestions offered.

This revised edition has been enlivened by the addition of a number of cartoons that illustrate the meaning of words in the adjacent text. Also, many thought-provoking review exercises have been substituted for lessons not definitely related to words previously introduced.

J.G.G.

Contents

[v]

[vi]

[vii]

Inventory Test 1

PRONUNCIATION

People are becoming extremely conscious of the importance of correct pronunciation. It is a healthy sign. With this realization, they are seeking all available means to eliminate from their speech as many of their mispronunciations as possible. Incorrect pronunciation invariably bespeaks carelessness or poor acquaintanceship with the dictionary, and will militate against any speaker.

Pronounce aloud the following **fifteen** words. Then check your results with the explanatory notes that accompany this test. Do not be surprised if you fail to hit the one-hundred-per-cent mark, for it is safe to say that not ten out of 100,000 readers of this test will receive a perfect score. You should obtain perfection, however, after the second or third attempt.

orgy	hosiery	inhospitable
comely	autopsy	formidable
respite	impotent	irreparable
renege	mayoralty	lamentable
zoology	chiropodist	remunerate

Notes

orgy (or'jee, not or'ghee)

"An excessive indulgence in some activity, as spending, speechmaking, etc.; a wild, drunken revel."

The g is sounded like the j in **jet**, not like the g in **get**.

Read aloud: There was an **orgy** of spending during the prosperity era.

An **orgy** of crime followed the last world war.

[1]

comely   (kum′ly, not comb′ly)

"Pleasing to the sight."

The first syllable should rhyme with **drum** and not with **foam**.

Read aloud: She was a **comely** person.

The **comely** attire of the speaker evoked many favorable remarks.

respite   (res′pit, not respite′)

"An interval of rest; a temporary suspension of labor or effort; a delay."

The first syllable is accented; the second syllable rhymes with **hit**.

Read aloud: The soldiers enjoyed the **respite** from fighting.

The governor seemed to receive no **respite** from his troubles.

renege   (reneeg′, not renague)

"To fail to follow suit when able to do so, in violation of the rules of the game."

The last syllable should rhyme with **league** and not with **plague**.

Read aloud: He was penalized because he **reneged.**

zoology   (zo ol′ ogy, not zoo ol′ ogy)

"The science that treats of animals or the animal kingdom."

Do not pronounce the first syllable **zoo.** The **zo** should rhyme with **flow.**

Read aloud: Many students have registered for the **zoology** course.

We visited the **zoological** garden.

hosiery   (ho′zher y, not hose′er y)

Note that the second syllable is pronounced **zher,** not **er.**

Read aloud: The **hosiery** sale attracted many purchasers.

autopsy   (au′topsy, not autop′sy)

Be sure to accent the first syllable and not the second.

Read aloud: The medical examiner performed the **autopsy.**

[2]

impotent (im'potent, not impo'tent)
"Lacking strength or power; weak."
Too frequently is this word accented on the second syllable, whereas to be correct the accent must be placed on the first syllable.

Read aloud: The policeman found himself **impotent** when attacked by the three criminals.

mayoralty (may'or al ty, not may or al'i ty)
"The position of mayor or his term of office."
This is a word of four syllables and not five. There is no letter **i** in it.

Read aloud: There are four candidates seeking the **mayoralty** of that city.

chiropodist (kye rop'o dist, not sher op'o dist)
"One who treats the ailments of the hands and feet, especially minor ailments."
Note that the first syllable rhymes with **eye.** Do not sound the **ch** as in **church.**

Read aloud: The **chiropodist** attributed the ailment to ill-fitting shoes.
He plans to study **chiropody.**

inhospitable (inhos'pitable, *Br.* inhospit'able)
"Not inclined to show welcome to guests; unkind."
Accent the second and not the third syllable.

Read aloud: We were disappointed at the **inhospitable** treatment we received.
Why did they act so **inhospitably?**

formidable (for'midable, not formid'able)
"Hard to accomplish; difficult to overcome."
To pronounce this word correctly, it will be necessary to accent the first syllable.

Read aloud: Building a subway will be a **formidable** undertaking.

irreparable (irrep'arable, not irrepair'able)
"Not capable of being repaired or remedied."
Accent the second syllable, not the third.

[3]

Read aloud: **Irreparable** damage was caused by the fire
His death was an **irreparable** loss to the country.

lamentable (lam'entable, not lament'able)
"Sad; mournful."
The first syllable, and not the second, requires the
accent.

> *Read aloud:* That family is in a **lamentable** state.
> He failed **lamentably** in his attempt to conquer the
> world.

remunerate (remu'nerate, not renew'mer ate)
"To reward; to pay for work."
Note that the second syllable is **mu**, not **nu**.

> *Read aloud:* We shall **remunerate** you for your services.

Inventory Test 2

VOCABULARY

Which one of the three words or expressions best defines the
boldface word? Write your answers on a sheet of paper.

1. **Stationary** means:
   a. Fixed in a certain place.
   b. Writing material.
   c. Not modern.
2. A **sedulous** person is one who:
   a. Is lazy.
   b. Is diligent.
   c. Is accustomed to sitting most of the time.
3. A **spurious** painting is one which:
   a. Is historically true.
   b. Has been stolen from an art gallery.
   c. Is not genuine.
4. A **missile** is:
   a. A prayerbook.
   b. A letter.
   c. An object thrown.

[4]

5. An **antidote** is:
   a. A remedy.
   b. A vegetable.
   c. A brief story intended to amuse.
6. A book is **extant** if it:
   a. Is still in existence.
   b. Is out of print.
   c. Is on the blacklist.
7. A **roster** is:
   a. A roll or list.
   b. A male fowl.
   c. A stage or pulpit used by a speaker.
8. A person may be called **ingenuous** if he:
   a. Has an inventive mind.
   b. Is without funds.
   c. Is frank or naïve.
9. To **elicit** a statement is to:
   a. Draw out or extract it.
   b. Declare it unlawful.
   c. Condemn it.
10. A **factotum** is a man who:
   a. Practices an art, such as painting or sculpture.
   b. Is too much interested in other people's business.
   c. Is employed to do all kinds of work.
11. You are the **cynosure** of the crowd if you:
   a. Are the object of dislike.
   b. Are the center of attraction.
   c. Are looked upon as having an easy position.
12. One is noted for his **temerity** if he:
   a. Is very fearful.
   b. Has an unreasonable contempt for danger.
   c. Uses abusive language.
13. A **cryptic** message is one which:
   a. Is very brief.
   b. Is of a secret nature.
   c. Is condemnatory in substance.

Inventory Test 3

WORDS CONFUSED

A common barrier for students and adults is the correct use of what might be called "word-pairs," that is, words which have a similarity of sound or appearance, such as **principal** and **principle**; **affect** and **effect**; **accede** and **exceed.** Too frequently is one used for the other. A little concentration and study will remedy this weakness.

In the following sentences there are *nine* words which are incorrectly used. Try to spot them and be ready to make the correct substitution. The assignment is a trifle difficult.

1. My test was not corrected because the writing was illegible.
2. The dome on the capitol building was struck by lightening.
3. Our governor is elected biannually.
4. The prisoner will be arranged in court tomorrow morning.
5. Mr. Jones, who was formally a college president, uses exceptionally fine English.
6. The order was that all soldiers' mail must be censured.
7. He was adverse to having martial music played at the exercises.
8. Three gifts, marked X, Y, and Z, were given respectively to John, Robert, and Henry.
9. His prophecy was that no one would proceed him in rank.
10. A treaty was effected with that country last year.
11. Many emigrants have settled in the capital of our state.
12. You will find the stationery on the mantel.
13. The interest of some members of the city counsel in our request was only affected.
14. He was debarred from the golf club because of his exceptionable remarks.
15. Our company has its full complement of men.

Inventory Test 4

SPELLING

Can You Find Them?

Read the following sentences at your natural rate of speed. Write on a separate sheet of paper each word that you think is misspelled. When the eleven sentences are finished, count the words you thought were not correctly spelled. If on the first reading you detected ten misspellings, consider yourself a very good speller. Do not be discouraged should you fail to receive a perfect score, because more than 95 per cent of the readers of this test will not find the ten words which are misspelled.

1. He was seized with a cramp while he was swimming.
2. The millionaire was harassed with requests for financial help.
3. Dissention was evident among the workers.
4. The sanitorium had many artifical poinsettas.
5. She put two spoonfuls of sugar in her coffee.
6. Mr. Brown was superseded by his brother.
7. He was embarrassed because he failed to fill out the questionaire.
8. The soldiers in the Phillipines were inoculated.
9. No one has ever benefitted from lieing.
10. The place could not accomodate the battalion.
11. Perhaps you will be in a state of ecstacy if you receive a perfect score on this test.

1

Prefixes

The following is a list of the most important prefixes used in forming English words. The letter "L" indicates that the prefix is from the Latin; the letter "G" indicates that the prefix is from the Greek.

Prefix	Meaning	Derivation
a or ab (L)	away from	avert, "to turn from"
		absolve, "to release from"
a or an (G)	not; destitute of	atheist, "one without God"
		anarchy, "want of government"
ambi (L)	around; both	ambidextrous, "able to use both hands well"
		ambiguous, "two meanings"
amphi (G)	around; both	amphitheatre, "a circular building with seats around an open place"
		amphibious, "able to live both on land and in water"
ante (L)	before	antecedent, "going before"
anti (G)	against	antiaircraft, "guns, etc., used in defense against aircraft"
bene (L)	well	benefactor, "one who performs kind deeds"
circum (L)	around	circumnavigate, "to sail around"
		circumference, "distance around a circle"
com (co, con, col, cor) (L)	together with	commiserate, "to sympathize with"
		consult, "to talk things over with"

Prefix	Meaning	Derivation
contra (L)	against	contradict, "to speak against"
de (L)	down from; away	deduct, "to take from" depart, "to go away"
dia (G)	through; between	diameter, "line from one side of a circle through center to the other side"
dis (di, dif) (L)	apart; away	dismiss, "to remove from" dissent, "to be of a different opinion"
e or ex (L & G)	out; out of	eject, "to cast out" exclude, "to shut out"
extra (L)	beyond; outside of	extraordinary, "beyond what is ordinary" extracurricular, "outside the regular course of study"
hyper (G)	above; beyond	hypercritical, "critical beyond reason"
hypo (G)	under	hypodermic, "under the skin"
in or en (L)	in; on; into	insert, "to put in" engrave, "to cut upon or in"
inter (L)	between; among	interpose, "to place between"
mal (L)	bad; evil	maladjusted, "poorly adjusted" malefactor, "a wrongdoer"
mis (L)	wrong	misconduct, "wrong conduct"
multi (L)	many	multicolored, "having many colors"
ob (L)	against	object, (v.) "to go against" obstruct, "to place against"
per (L)	through	pervade, "to spread throughout"

Prefix	Meaning	Derivation
peri (G)	around	**perimeter,** "distance around a surface or figure"
post (L)	after	**postscript,** "something written later"
		post mortem, "after death"
pre (L)	before	**precede,** "to go before"
		predict, "to tell beforehand"
pro (L)	for; forward; forth	**pronoun,** "for a noun"
		progress, (*v*.) "to go forward"
re (L)	back; again	**reread,** "to read again"
		recall, "to call back"
retro (L)	backward	**retroactive,** "acting back"
		retrogress, "to move backward"
se (L)	aside; away; apart	**secede,** "to draw away from"
		seduce, "to lead away from right"
sub (L)	under	**subway,** "underground passage"
		subvert, "to undermine"
super (L)	over; above	**supervise,** "to oversee"
		superabundance, "above the amount needed"
syn or **sym** (G)	with; together	**synchronize,** "to agree with (in regard to time, etc.)"
		sympathize, "to share a feeling with"
trans (L)	over; beyond; across	**transatlantic,** "across the Atlantic"
		transgress, "to go beyond (a limit or bound)"

2

Verbs That Will Prove Useful

Study the definitions of the following verbs in order to be prepared to do the lesson on the next page.

debar	To exclude.
elude	To avoid cleverly.
abate	To lessen.
refute	To prove to be false.
obsess	To fill the mind of.
retract	To take back.
impeach	To accuse.
transmit	To send out.
emulate	To imitate.
frustrate	To defeat or disappoint.
supersede	To take the place of.
subsidize	To help with a grant of money.

Completion Exercise

Fill each blank with a word from the above list to complete the meaning of the sentence. The past tense may be used if necessary.

1. The boy _____ the blow that was directed at him.
2. Our picnic plans were _____ by heavy showers.
3. The prisoner refused to _____ his confession.
4. Try to _____ the style of the great writers.
5. He was _____ with the thought that people disliked him.
6. They were _____ from the organization because of their subversive activities.
7. A group of citizens have agreed to _____ the symphony orchestra.
8. The professor failed to _____ his ideas to the class.

3

Verb Exercise

Your Answer, Please

What is your answer to each of the following questions
which pertain to words found in the preceding lesson?

1. When is a statement **refuted**?
2. When does a football player **elude** an opposing player?
3. When are taxes **abated**?
4. When is a project **subsidized**?
5. When is a disease **transmitted**?
6. When are plans **frustrated**?
7. When is a judge **impeached**?
8. When is a person **superseded** in office?
9. When is an offer **retracted**?
10. When is one **obsessed** with an idea?
11. When is one **debarred** from society?
12. When is a work **emulated**?

Exercise

1. Construct original sentences with:
   - a. The noun form of **refute**.
   - b. The adjectival form of **elude**.
   - c. The noun form of **retract**.
2. Place the following in original sentences:
   - a. **frustrated hopes**
   - b. **elusive answer**
   - c. **irrefutable testimony**
   - d. **unabated enthusiasm**
3. How does **elude** differ from **delude**?
4. Give three verbs which contain the prefix **trans**.

4

Root Words

There is every reason to believe that the student, whether or not he has studied Latin, may be somewhat skeptical about the frequent allusions to the importance of acquiring a knowledge of the basic Latin roots. To be sure, he is entitled to his doubt. He has to be shown, and it devolves upon the author and the teacher to present unmistakable proof that Latin forms the core of the majority of our English words.

An appropriate word, therefore, to start this series of lessons may be the Latin word **specto**, which is associated with "seeing or looking."

Inasmuch as the stems of verbs are taken from the present tense and the past participle, these two forms will be given for each verb studied in the lessons on "Root Words." In the case of nouns, the basic stem is usually found in the form for the genitive (or possessive) case. Both the nominative and genitive cases will be given for nouns.

specto *(pres. tense)*, **spectatus** *(past participle)*, "to look at"

The stem is ordinarily obtained by dropping the letter **o** from the first form or the **us** from the past participle.

The stem of this root word is **spect** or **spectat**.

Note how the meaning "to look at" is woven into each of the following words:

aspect,	a view (a looking at something)
inspect,	to look into (a looking into something for the purpose of examining it)
expect,	to look for
specter,	a ghost; a visible, disembodied spirit
suspect, (*v.*)	to look upon with distrust
prospect, (*n.*)	outlook for the future
spectacle,	a scene; a show
spectacles,	eyeglasses to help a person's sight
spectator,	one who looks on; an observer
speculate,	to look at a proposition before coming to a decision

spectacular, exciting wonder and admiration by unusual display

Let us take two rather uncommon words in order to see how easily they can be understood by examining their parts, namely, the prefix and the stem or root. The words are:

circumspect and **retrospect**

The prefix **circum** means "around"; the stem **spect,** "to look." When a person plans to rob a store, does he break into it suddenly and without making any observations? No siree. The intruder approaches the scene, lingers about for a time, looks up and down the street to be sure there is no one in the vicinity to interfere with his job. When everything seems safe, he begins his wicked mission. Yes, he is very careful, and that is the meaning of **circumspect,** "cautious; careful."

In **retrospect,** the prefix **retro** means "back" and the stem **spect,** "to look"; when united, we have the denotation "a looking back on things past."

5

Words Frequently Confused

This lesson should accomplish a twofold purpose. It should familiarize the student with the difference that exists between the words of each pair, and it should be instrumental in increasing his vocabulary.

censor One who critically examines books, plays, mail, etc., for moral and protective purposes.

censure (*v.*) To criticize adversely; to condemn as wrong.

One statement in the soldier's mail was deleted by the **censor.**

The boy was **censured** for his lack of good manners.

The officers were **censured** for their inefficiency.

(Censure is pronounced **sen sher.** Be sure to sound the **sh.)**

[14]

| flout | To treat with scorn or contempt. |
| flaunt | To display in a showy or ostentatious manner. |

Children should not **flout** the advice of their parents or elders.

She always **flaunted** her jewelry before her friends.

Do not **flaunt** your knowledge either publicly or privately.

| eminent | Famous; distinguished. |
| imminent | Threatening to occur in the immediate future. |

He comes from an **eminent** family.

The dark clouds told us that a storm was **imminent**.

Though the two countries do not seem to agree on major problems, war is by no means **imminent**.

| alumni | Male graduates |
| alumnae | Female graduates. |

The last syllable of **alumni** should rhyme with **die**; the last syllable of **alumnae** should rhyme with **bee**.

6

Pronunciation

It may be necessary for the student to give more than average study to the pronunciations of the words in the following list. Some of these words are mispronounced more frequently than they are pronounced correctly.

1. alias	An assumed name.
2. viscid	Sticky; gluey.
3. flaccid	Flabby; limp.
4. salient	Prominent; conspicuous.
5. impotent	Without power; helpless.
6. poinsettia	Plant with small, greenish flowers and large red leaves.
7. maraschino	Sweet drink made from small black cherries.

8. machination — A scheming against authority; an evil plot.
9. remuneration — Reward; repayment.
10. boutonniere — Flower worn in a buttonhole.

The Correct Forms

1. alias — ay'le us, not uh lye'us.
2. viscid — vis'id, not vis'kid.
3. flaccid — flak'sid, not flas id.
4. salient — say'le unt, not sail' yunt.
5. impotent — im'potent, not impo'tent.
6. poinsettia — poin set'i uh, not poin set'uh.
7. maraschino — mar uh skee'no, not mar uh shee'no.
8. machination — mak in nay'shun, not mash in ay'shun.
9. remuneration — re mew ner ay'shun, not re new'mer ray'shun.
10. boutonniere — boo tuh nyair', not boo tah neer'.

Completion Exercise

Fill each blank with a word from the above list to complete the sentence, and read aloud each completed sentence.

1. Every man wore a _____.
2. Mr. Kay, _____ Mr. Brown, was taken into custody by the police last week.
3. The leader would not tolerate any political_____.
4. Lack of exercise made his muscles _____.
5. He realized that he was _____ against such great opposition.
6. What was his _____ objection?

7

Words Taken from Achievement Tests

Many of the following words taken from various national vocabulary tests proved difficult to students in both colleges and high schools. Focus your attention upon the various definitions, and you will find the succeeding exercise both interesting and instructive.

pallid	Pale; lacking color.
squalid	Filthy; wretched.
titanic	Having enormous size.
pedantic	Displaying one's knowledge in a show-off way.
quixotic	Visionary; not practical.
palpable	Obvious; capable of being seen or felt.
equivocal	Having two or more meanings; doubtful.
chimerical	Imaginary; unreal.
meticulous	Excessively careful about details.
reciprocal	Given in return; mutual.
subversive	Destructive; tending to overthrow.
tumultuous	Disorderly; greatly disturbed.
irksome	Dull; tiresome; tedious.
converge	To meet in a point; to come together.
autonomy	Self-government; independence.
dispirited	Discouraged; disheartened.
remorse	Distress, excited by a sense of guilt.
verbose	Using too many words; wordy.
implicate	To involve; to entangle.
sanguinary	Bloody; attended with bloodshed.

Completion Exercise

Fill each blank with a word from the preceding list to complete the meaning of the sentence. The past tense of a verb may be used if necessary.

1. If a wrong were committed which would be easily detected, you might describe it as a _____ wrong.

2. If a sentence or statement can be interpreted in more than one way, it could be called _____.

3. If a person likes to display his knowledge, you might say he is _____.

4. If hundreds of lives were lost as a result of an explosion it could be called a _____ disaster.

5. If one's countenance lost its color through fear or illness, you might apply the adjective _____ to describe it.

[17]

6. If you were to journey through the slum sections of a large city, no doubt you would say that _____ conditions existed there.

7. If pamphlets are distributed in which the people are urged to rise up against their government, such material could rightly be called _____.

8. If you were asked to write the translation of twenty pages of Latin, you might find the assignment very _____.

9. If the people of a country wish to govern themselves, they are seeking _____.

10. If a speaker uses many words and repetitions, you would be justified in saying that he is too _____ to be interesting.

11. If strikers and non-strikers clashed and many were injured, the fight might be described as a _____ conflict.

12. If two or more streets met, you may say that they _____.

13. If someone declared that you were one of those who started the riot, it would _____ you.

14. If the members of the football team took defeat so seriously that they were sad and silent, they might be described as being somewhat _____.

ELUDE

8

Review

This exercise is based on words found in previous lessons. What is your answer for each question?

Quiz

1. When is a storm **imminent**?
2. Should a person **flaunt** his intellectual ability?
3. What is the sound of the last syllable in **boutonniere**?
4. Why are not **verbose** speakers popular?
5. Should we try to **emulate** the work of successful people?
6. In what respect is a student with a good vocabulary **remunerated**? Give two reasons.
7. Does the first syllable in **flaccid** rhyme with the first syllable in **machination**? Pronounce both.
8. Would you care to associate with a person of **subversive** ideas?

True or False

Correct the false statements in this exercise.

1. As a rule, long-winded speakers are **irksome**.
2. An **elusive** runner is an asset to a football team.
3. Even though you know you are wrong, you should not make a **retraction**.
4. Humility was not a **salient** characteristic of President Lincoln.
5. **Squalid** conditions do not add to the scenic beauty of any city.
6. One reasons better after his anger has **abated**.
7. All who commit unlawful acts are **remorseful**.
8. Great statesmen are not defeated by **frustrations**.
9. **Censurable** conduct should not be tolerated.
10. That two and two make four cannot be **refuted**.

Root word. *Pan* (*Gr.*), all

Research Exercise

Prove that the following words are associated in meaning with the above root word. It will be necessary for you to consult the dictionary for the correct definitions.

1. panacea
2. panoply
3. pantheon
4. Pan American

5. panegyric
6. pantheism
7. panorama
8. pandemonium

9

Word Origins

The student who has never plunged into the history and origin of words will find the experience most delightful. The study of root words alleviates the burden formerly placed on one's memory and enables him to remember the meanings of words with greater confidence and permanency. Delving into word-history will produce these two results and also prove far more entertaining than any phase of word study presented so far.

abundant

To the ancients, nothing signified greatness in number or quantity more than did the waves of the sea. To them, the waves were infinite: they were numberless. **Abundant** is composed of the Latin words **ab**, "from," and **unda**, "wave." The basic form is the latter. From these few sentences the student can readily understand the present-day meaning of **abundant**, "plentiful; a large supply." No doubt the boldface words will now mean more to the student than formerly.

Other Words Derived from *Unda*

1. He is suffering from **undulant** fever. (A malady in which the temperature rises and falls like the waves.)

[20]

2. The author referred to the **undulating** scenery of the New England countryside. (Resembling the up-and-down appearance of waves.)
3. The city was **inundated**. (Was under the waves; was flooded.)
4. It was a **redundant** statement. (Note the **unda** in this word. It was an overlapping or unnecessary statement. We do not have two waves coinciding with each other.)

candidate

Before the days of the radio, the telephone, television, or printing, the only manner in which a Roman could "broadcast" or signify his intention of seeking a civic position was by the garb he wore. The aspirants for office would appear publicly in long, flowing white togas, or robes. **Candidate** is derived from the Latin **candidus,** which means "white." What is a **candid** statement? Is it not one that is frank, honest, and truthful? Does not the color "white" symbolize honesty, purity, and truth?

10

Vocabulary Game

I. *DATE* WORDS

Vocabulary work can be made interesting as well as profitable by linking the game or quiz element with various exercises. Every person likes a challenge that will test his mental ability. For the following sentences you are to select a word that ends in **date** which will conform or agree with what is suggested. At the end of the exercise will be found the first letters of the desired words. They **are not arranged** according to the order of the sentences.

1. The first **date** refers to an aspirant for an office.
2. The next **date** describes a maiden who is quiet and serious.
3. The third **date** is an order or authoritative command.

4. The fourth **date** refers to a merger or the uniting of two companies.

5. This **date** means to shed light upon a subject or plan.

6. This **date** may be what one would like to do when his checking account is very low and a large bill is due.

7. This **date** frightens or threatens.

8. The eighth **date** sees one's debts settled.

9. This **date** may be used in reference to a wall or building that is crumbling from lack of care.

10. This **date** is used when talking about a city that has suffered greatly from torrential rains and floods.

11. The last **date** refers to what a hotel manager endeavors to do when there is a great demand for reservations.

(First letters: **c, i, i, s, c, p, a, l, e, m, d.**)

II. *RATE* WORDS

On a separate sheet of paper copy the following sentences and fill each blank with a word that ends in **rate** (you may need to use the past tense) to complete the meaning of the sentence. The first letter of the required word is given.

1. Let me **e**_____ his many fine qualities.

2. His spending is not **c**_____ with his earnings, and that is the cause of the trouble.

3. Try to **i**_____ these words in your everyday conversation.

4. The cloth was **s**_____ with kerosene.

5. We must **p**_____ the paper in order to put it in our notebooks.

6. Did the storm **o**_____ the footprints of the burglar?

7. The buildings are beginning to be **d**_____ because of age.

8. He is **t**_____ in his use of food and drink.

9. The suspect was **e**_____ of the charge.

11

Clinching Test No. 1

I. Matching

For each definition in Column 1 below, find in Column 2 the word it defines and place its number in the blank preceding the definition.

Column 1	*Column 2*
1. _____ pale	1. flout
2. _____ flabby	2. pallid
3. _____ to involve	3. squalid
4. _____ obvious	4. flaccid
5. _____ to treat with contempt	5. verbose
6. _____ a cure-all	6. implicate
7. _____ filthy	7. subversive
8. _____ to overflow; to deluge	8. panacea
9. _____ using too many words	9. palpable
10. _____ destructive	10. inundate

II. Completion Exercise

Fill each blank with a word or expression that will complete the meaning of the sentence.

1. **Impotent** is accented on the _____ syllable.
2. The Latin word **specto** means _____.
3. Two English words which stem from **specto** are _____ and _____.
4. A synonym and an antonym for **dispirited** are _____ and _____.
5. **Censor,** the verb, means _____ and not "to condemn."
6. Girl graduates of a college are called _____.
7. The root word of **avert** and **subvert** is _____, which means _____.

[23]

III

Correct each statement that is false:

1. **Censure** and **censor** are not synonyms.
2. There is no such word as **renumeration**.
3. The **ch** in **machination** is sounded like the **ch** in **ma-chine**.
4. **Viscid** is pronounced **vis'id**.
5. **Refute** means more than "to contradict."
6. **Debar** may be defined as "to deprive a lawyer of his legal status and privileges."

12

Vocabulary Exercise—Adjectives

Here is another list of adjectives which should be added to your supply. Strive to use them in your active vocabulary.

supine	Listless; inactive; lying flat on back.
pungent	Stinging; caustic.
faltering	Hesitating; moving unsteadily.
detestable	Hateful; much disliked.
legitimate	Lawful; rightful.
dominant	Most influential; controlling; ruling.
punitive	Concerned with punishment.
scathing	Bitterly severe; scorching.
inordinate	Excessive; unrestrained.
seditious	Stirring up discontent or rebellion.
inevitable	Certain to happen.
contemptible	Deserving of scorn; despicable.

Completion Exercise

I. Fill each blank with the word that will make the sentence correct:

1. An antonym for **supine** is _____.
2. The verb form of **dominant** is _____.

[24]

3. A synonym for **scathing** is _____.

4. The noun form for **seditious** is _____.

II. Explain the following:

    1. He is a **dominant** figure in our city.

    2. Death of the body is **inevitable**.

    3. That their hopes were **faltering** was evident to all.

    4. A **punitive** army was despatched to the border.

    5. His **inordinate** appetite played havoc with his weight.

13

Review of Adjectives

I. How Would You Say It?

What word from the previous lesson would you use:

    1. To describe a very mean act?

    2. To describe demands that are out of proportion to reason?

    3. To describe a voice that is weak and stammering?

    4. To describe a very sharp odor?

    5. To describe a wish that surpasses all your other wishes?

    6. To describe a very severe scolding or reprimand?

    7. To describe a ruler who lets others dictate to him?

    8. To describe a rightful claim to certain property?

    9. To describe a look that is full of hate or meanness?

    10. To describe a group that strives to produce a revolution?

    11. To describe measures that entail punishment?

    12. To describe a result that is bound to come?

II. Related Exercise

To which word in the preceding lesson is each boldface word related? Explain the meaning of each sentence.

    1. The lawyer questioned the **legitimacy** of my ownership of the property.

    2. You cannot break nature's laws with **impunity**.

    3. We had a feeling of **contempt** for all who sought to undermine our government.

4. She seemed to be able to **dominate** the other members of the family.

5. Their courage began to **falter** as the hour for the attack approached.

6. The speaker **scathingly** attacked the administration for its inactivity.

7. He who idles away his time in school or college will **inevitably** regret it in later years.

8. The leaders of the **sedition** were apprehended by the police.

9. The children in the neighborhood seem to be **inordinately** happy.

14

Root Words

A few decades ago Latin and even Greek were found in nearly every secondary-school curriculum. Many students registered for these subjects because they were college entrance requirements. But in those days neither the importance of an effective vocabulary nor a systematic approach to increasing one's word supply was sufficiently emphasized.

Today, inasmuch as these ancient languages are not required college entrance subjects, there is a radical decrease in the number of high school students enrolled in these classes. But although there is unmistakable recognition by the students and faculty of the importance of a practical and fluent vocabulary, there is no definite mode of instruction. The work is sporadic and incidental, and the difficulty is accentuated because of the large number of students who do not possess even a slight knowledge of Latin. As to Greek, this subject has been withdrawn from the curriculum of nearly every high school in the country.

A knowledge of either or both of these languages would obviate the necessity for memorizing all definitions. The meanings of many words would be known or approximately known if the root forms were recognized.

For example, a knowledge of the Latin word **vertere**, which means "to turn" and whose past participle is **versus**, will enable the student to see more clearly, understand better, and remember longer the meanings of such words as:

avert	subvert	diverse
advert	vertex	converse
divert	vertical	inverse
invert	vertebra	perverse
revert	vertigo	traverse
pervert	adverse	reversible
controvert	aversion	subversive

Many other derivatives of **vertere** could be given, but the number of examples listed should furnish conclusive proof of the relationship between Latin and English.

Throughout this book will be found lessons that contain some of the basic Latin and Greek roots. In them the student will receive at least some knowledge of the two languages which have contributed so many words to the English tongue.

15

Pronunciation

WORDS HAVING TWO PRONUNCIATIONS

The second edition of *Webster's New International Dictionary* (1934) and *Webster's New Collegiate Dictionary* (1949) incorporated pronunciations which prior to these dates were considered incorrect. Most of the added forms are recorded as secondary. If possible, one should strive to use the preferred or first pronunciation. How do you naturally pronounce the following?

inquiry	ally (*n.*)	infantile
pianist	valet	illustrate
economic	gala	juvenile

virile   Forceful; vigorous.
senile   Characteristic of old age.

aspirant   One who seeks a position or honor.
acclimate   To become accustomed to a climate or condi-
              tion.
despicable   Mean; contemptible.

inertia   Lack of activity; sluggishness.
alienate   To cause to turn away; to estrange.
centenary   A period of one hundred years.
obligatory   Required; binding in law or conscience.
sacrilegious Profane; treating sacred things irreverently.

Check Your Answers

	Preferred	*Secondary*
inquiry	inquye'ry	in'query
pianist	peean'ist	pee'anist
economic	ee konom'ik	ek onom'ik
ally (*n.*)	a lye'	al'eye
valet	val'et	val'ay
gala	gay'luh	gal'uh
infantile	in'fan tile	in'fan till
illustrate	il'lustrate	illus'trate
juvenile	jew'ven ill	jew'ven ile
virile	vir'ill	vye'rill
senile	see'nile	see'nill
aspirant	aspye'rant	as'pirant
acclimate	aklye'mit	ak'luhmate
despicable	des'picable	despik'able
inertia	in err'shuh	in err'shi uh
alienate	ail'yen ate	ay'lee un ate
centenary	sen'tenary	senten'ary
obligatory	oblig'atory	ob'ligatory
sacrilegious	sak ruh lee'jus	sak ruh lij'us

Completion Exercise

Fill each blank with a word taken from the preceding lists
to complete the sentence. The past tense of the verb may be
used if necessary.

1. Deformity can be the result of _____ paralysis.

[28]

2. We should have more _____ books in our school library.

3. He soon became _____ to his new position.

4. His bitter remarks _____ many of his followers.

5. The chairman refused to answer my _____.

6. Who is the leading _____ for that office?

7. He made a _____ attempt to introduce new legislation for the improvement of our schools.

8. We overlooked his _____ peculiarities.

9. The judge upbraided him for his _____ act.

10. Attendance at school is _____.

11. The destruction of the church property was _____.

12. We shall celebrate the _____ of his birth next week.

13. England was our _____ during the two world wars.

14. It was a _____ occasion.

15. He was considered great even in the estimation of his _____.

16. The _____ of the people was discouraging to the leaders.

16

Vocabulary

I. Multiple-Choice Exercise

1. If you are **prodigal,** does it mean that you are:
   (1) very extravagant, (2) economical, or (3) very well known?

2. If you **conform to the rules of the** club, does it mean that you:
   (1) disregard them, (2) obey them, or (3) wish to strengthen them?

3. If you have a **chronic** ailment, does it mean that:
   (1) it is very severe, (2) it pertains to the heart, or (3) you have had it for a long time?

4. If you met a **diffident** person, would he be:
   (1) an unusual one, (2) very haughty, or (3) lacking in confidence?

5. If your brother were **impetuous**, would he be:
(1) fearful, (2) impulsive, or (3) a lengthy speaker?

6. If you were accused of being **parsimonious**, would it mean that you:
(1) were close in spending money, (2) were very careful, or (3) liked farming?

7. If you **deprecate** the use of long words, does it mean that you:
(1) try to cultivate them, (2) disapprove of them, or (3) encourage adopting them?

8. If you are **abstemious** at the table, does it mean that you:
(1) overeat, (2) dislike food, or (3) are moderate in eating and drinking?

9. If you are surrounded by **amiable** persons, does it mean that they are:
(1) kind-hearted, (2) unfriendly, or (3) elderly?

10. If you used **ambiguous** language, would it be:
(1) intelligible, (2) difficult to understand, or (3) abusive?

11. If you were dissatisfied with your **emolument**, does it mean that you:
(1) disliked the position, (2) thought you were underpaid, or (3) objected to being transferred?

12. If you rendered a **creditable** account of your activities, does it mean that your report was:
(1) deserving of praise, (2) a comprehensive report, or (3) capable of being believed?

II. Exercise

1. Give two synonyms for **parsimonious**.

2. Construct a sentence containing the adjective **conformable**.

3. Write two words which begin with **ambi**.

4. Give three words which contain the syllable **chron**.

5. Name two synonyms for **prodigal**.

17

Synonyms

allay	apathy	dauntless	harmonize
deface	fusion	exasperate	irrelevant
allege	adverse	vivacious	apprehensive

I. Substitution Exercise

Select from the above list a word that is a synonym for each boldface word in the following sentences. The past tense of a verb may be used if necessary.

1. The children **spoiled** the building with chalk-writing.
2. The judge rendered an **unfavorable** opinion.
3. The colors in the room do not seem to **agree**.
4. The poor condition of our schools may be attributed to the **indifference** of the public.
5. His remarks were **impertinent** to the case.
6. There will be a **union** of the two political parties next year.
7. We endeavored to **calm** the fears of his parents.
8. She was the most **active** member of the class.
9. It was **claimed** that the goods were removed during the night.
10. We were **vexed** at the childish complaints of the officials.
11. A criminal is always **afraid** of being captured.
12. To accomplish such a dangerous mission it was necessary to select **brave** men.

II. Exercise

1. Construct a sentence with an antonym of **vivacious**.
2. What do you mean by **relevant** testimony?
3. Give three definitions for **apprehend**.
4. What are the noun-forms of: **allege; adverse; harmonize?**

Words from Achievement Tests

Selection Exercise

quell	ramify	paragon	aggrandize
vaunt	perfidy	asunder	blithesome
influx	rescind	bereft	accentuate

Select from the above groups the word which can best be substituted for each of the boldface words or phrases in the following sentences. The words have been taken from achievement test lists.

1. In his anger he tore the book **into pieces.**
2. The traitor was hanged for his **treachery,** his disloyalty to his country.
3. The police were summoned **to put an end to** the riot.
4. She has a very **cheerful** nature.
5. Many of the words **branch out** from the root of that word.
6. As a result of the fire the child **was deprived** of his parents.
7. As you acquire a greater knowledge of words, you gradually sense a **pouring in** of confidence into your speech.
8. He would stop short of nothing in order to **increase** his financial resources.
9. He liked to **speak boastfully of** his college achievements.
10. He was considered a **model of perfection** in diplomatic circles.
11. Because of the lawlessness that followed the football victory, the president of the college decided to **cancel** our permission to attend the game in New York the following week.
12. The shrubs and flowers which were recently planted **make more prominent** the beauty of the campus.

19

Word Origins

bedlam

In the fifteenth century there was in London a hospital for the insane, St. Mary of Bethlehem. Perhaps through carelessness, the name was gradually contracted to *Bethlem, Bedlem,* and finally *Bedlam.* As time went on, this became the term for any institution for people of unsound and disordered minds. Today, **bedlam** refers not to a hospital, but to the uproar and confusion that are associated with a place for lunatics.

daisy

This word, which is of Anglo-Saxon origin, has a rather beautiful and appropriate association. It means "day's eye." Get a mental picture of the common daisy. You see a yellow disk surrounded by white rays. The yellow heart of the flower suggests the sun and the white fringe its rays.

curfew

The French **couvrefeu,** from which **curfew** is derived, means "utensil to cover the fire." It was primarily a signal given to the soldiers during the Middle Ages to extinguish the camp fires as evening approached so that the glare would not be seen by the enemy and thereby indicate the position of the camp. With the heat of the fire gone, the soldiers would wrap themselves in their blankets and retire for the night. In some places today a **curfew** is sounded at 9 P.M. as a signal for children to be off the streets and in their homes.

idiot

You were either a soldier or an "idiot," according to the ancient Greeks. With them there were only two classifications: the military forces and private citizens. The word they applied to the latter was **idiotes.** Why any man would spurn the chance to serve his country by taking up arms was difficult for them to understand. To them, one who chose the life of a private citizen was odd and foolish—which meaning is somewhat allied to our interpretation of the word **idiot.**

20

Vocabulary Game

I. *GATE* WORDS

The reader is asked to marshal his supply of words that end in **gate** to enable him to do justice to this exercise. In the following sentences, you are to substitute for the words in bold type a word ending in **gate** which will retain the meaning of the sentence. The past tense of a verb may be used if necessary.

1. We shall **look into** this matter at once.
2. The lawyer **asked questions of** the witness.
3. He was sent as our **representative** to the meeting.
4. This affair will have to be **settled by the court.**
5. The soil must be **watered** in order to get better crops.
6. Every evening we would **get together** in the library.
7. The judge refused to **lessen** the sentence.
8. The boys and girls in that school are **in different classrooms.**
9. You will have to **remove** the objectionable passages from your book.
10. The missionaries are trying to **spread** the faith in the Orient.
11. She should try to **conquer** her desire for such costly clothes.
12. He was **severely criticized** for his caustic remarks.

(The first letters of the words required, though not presented in the order of the sentences, are: **s, s, c, c, i, i, i, d, l, m, e, p.**)

II. USEFUL *GATES*

Can you associate a word that ends in **gate** with each of the following? The first letter of the required word is given in parentheses.

1. A **gate** which increases in length. **(e)**
2. A **gate** which disinfects. **(f)**
3. A **gate** of self-denial. **(a)**
4. A **gate** given to traveling by water. **(n)**

[34]

5. A **gate** that proclaims and publishes. **(p)**
6. A **gate** of many colors. **(v)**
7. A **gate** which repeals laws or privileges. **(a)**
8. A **gate** full of wrinkles. **(c)**
9. A **gate** which sends people into exile. **(r)**
10. A **gate** which binds morally or pledges. **(o)**

21

Clinching Test No. 2

I. Substitution Exercise

Substitute in each of the following expressions a word found in the preceding lessons that will be synonymous with the boldface word. The first letter of the required word is given.

1. an **unrestrained** appetite   i_____
2. a **controlling** position   d_____
3. an **unavoidable** failure   i_____
4. a **listless** person   s_____
5. an **evasive** answer   e_____
6. a **lawful** excuse   l_____
7. an **extravagant** spender   p_____
8. a **vigorous** speech   v_____
9. a **fearless** boy   d_____
10. a **repealed** law   r_____

II. Completion Exercise

allay	conform	punitive	alienate
quell	bedlam	influx	ambiguous
deface	chronic	diffident	irrelevant

Fill each blank with a word from the above list to complete the meaning of the sentence.

1. The pupils were asked not to _____ any property during the Halloween period.

2. The judge stated that the testimony was _____ to the case.

3. More _____ laws relative to auto speeding should be enacted.

4. One's spending should _____ to his income.

5. You will _____ many of your followers if you deliver that speech.

6. _____ broke loose among the students when their team won the game.

7. He was too _____ to ask for an increase in salary.

8. An effective vocabulary will result in an _____ of confidence.

9. She is a _____ sufferer from headaches.

10. The police were called to _____ the riot.

11. The salve seemed to _____ the pain.

12. His statement was so _____ that it was difficult to know what he really planned to do.

PUNGENT

[36]

22

Review

This exercise is based on words found on pages 24-35.

The Question Is

1. What is an **inordinate** appetite?
2. What is considered **irrelevant** testimony?
3. When is a person afflicted with **inertia**?
4. What is a **dominant** personality?
5. When is an uprising **quelled**?
6. When is a teacher likely to become **exasperated**?
7. What is your definition of an **impetuous** child?
8. When are friends **alienated**?
9. What is **adverse** criticism?

Explanation Required

What is the meaning of each of the following sentences?

1. His voice **faltered** when he spoke of the death of his dear son.
2. The youngsters were indeed **vivacious**.
3. There are times when parents should adopt **punitive** measures with their children.
4. His action received a **scathing** editorial in yesterday's paper.
5. Some people are **prodigal** spenders.
6. She is the most **diffident** girl in our class.
7. The boys made a **virile** attempt to win the game.
8. Children should not **deface** property.
9. There was a great **influx** of skilled mechanics into our city last year.
10. The colors in this room do not **harmonize**.

23

Verbs That Will Prove Useful

recoil	To draw back as in fear or disgust; to spring back.
digress	To get away from the main subject in speech or writing.
merit	To deserve; to earn by service or performance.
flounder	To struggle about without making much progress.
modify	To change somewhat; to alter.
rectify	To correct.
enervate	To weaken; to deprive of nerve or strength.
dominate	To be the ruling force in; to have a commanding position over.
transgress	To go beyond the limits of.
revivify	To give new life to; to restore to life.
repudiate	To reject; to disown.
retaliate	To return like for like, usually evil for evil.

Completion Exercise

Fill each blank with a verb taken from the above list to complete the meaning of the sentence. The past tense may, if necessary, be used.

1. The sergeant seemed to _____ his authority.
2. We _____ with fear at the thought of the accident.
3. One should never let fear _____ him.
4. All agreed that the speaker _____ too much during his talk.
5. The extremely hot and humid weather _____ the workers.
6. Efforts are being made to _____ interest in inter-class sports.
7. His excellent record proved that he _____ the promotion.
8. The speaker _____ for words because of lack of confidence in his own ability.
9. The clerk _____ the mistake on my monthly bill.

[38]

10. The lawyer tried to _____ the statement made by the witness.

11. He was asked to _____ the speech before delivering it.

24

Verb Exercise

I. Quiz

What word from the preceding list would you use:

1. To imply that you would cast aside the offer for your property?

2. To say that the act was committed to repay an injury that was done to you?

3. To convey the idea that our school spirit has returned?

4. To say that you were filled with fear at the thought of taking the final examinations?

5. To convey the idea that the small nations are under the power of a certain large country?

6. To imply that the person did not obey nature's laws?

7. To say that the mischievous boy deserved the punishment he received?

8. To say that the speaker had to grope for words?

9. To say that too much athletic practice is weakening?

10. To convey the thought that the speaker did not stick to his subject?

11. To imply that the judge would not change the verdict?

12. To state that you would be willing to see that the error was corrected?

II. General Exercise

Explain the meaning of each of the following sentences. It will then be to your advantage to construct original sentences with the boldface words.

1. The boat began to **flounder** when it lost its rudder.

2. Defacing the property was a **retaliatory** act.

3. He was debarred from society for his many **transgressions**.

4. That country's **repudiation** of her debts evoked much criticism.

5. A very busy person should have some **digression** from his business activities.

6. The president of the organization would not permit any **modification** of his report.

25

Pronunciation

The words that follow, although they are with a few exceptions of the everyday variety, present pronunciation difficulties. The correct pronunciations can be learned with a little effort. Study the meanings as well as the correct pronunciations of the ten words.

regime	A system of government, rule, or management.
venial	Not seriously wrong; excusable.
hosiery	Stockings.
meringue	A mixture of beaten white of egg and sugar.
fricassee	Meat stewed in gravy or soup.
amicable	Friendly; peaceable.
auxiliary	Helping; assisting.
chastisement	Punishment.
inexplicable	Cannot be explained; unexplainable.
sarsaparilla	A cooling drink made from the root of a tropical plant.

To enable the student to learn the correct pronunciations with a minimum of study, the phonetic forms will be used whenever it is deemed practicable.

regime	ray zheem', not rej'im. Regimen, a synonym for **regime**, has the Anglicized pronunciation: rej'uh min.

venial	vee'ne ul. Note that there are three syllables.
hosiery	hoe'zher y. Give a zh sound to si.
meringue	muh rang'. No doubt the students find greater relish in the meaning and taste of meringue than in its pronunciation.
fricassee	frik uh see'. The first syllable is pronunced frik, not frig, as is frequently heard.
amicable	am'uh ka b'l. The first syllable receives the accent.
auxiliary	aug zil'yuh ry. This is a word of four syllables, not five.
chastisement	chas'tiz ment. Accent the first syllable, not the second.
inexplicable	in eks'plik uh b'l. Apparently this word would be easier to pronounce if it were accented on the third syllable, but the dictionaries still accent the second syllable.
sarsaparilla	sar'suh pah ril uh. Five syllables. Do not say sas'puh ril'uh.

26

Words Frequently Confused

UNINTERESTED AND DISINTERESTED

What do you know of the word **uninterested** and its perplexing relative, **disinterested**? The same question might be asked about the other words in the following groups, all of which have some degree of difficulty. A careful study of the definitions of the words in this lesson should remedy any lack of knowledge regarding their correct usage.

If a person shows no interest in what is being said or done, if he appears bored, then he may be described as being **uninterested**.

If he is much interested in what is taking place and displays no partiality or favoritism, he may be said to be **disinterested**.

The student failed in chemistry because he was **uninterested** in the subject.

He finds all athletic activities **uninteresting.**

Every judge should be **disinterested** in the case or trial that he is conducting.

A football referee should be **disinterested** in the outcome of the contest at which he is officiating.

observation   Habit of noting details; act of seeing or noticing.

observance   The practice of taking notice of a rule, custom, holiday, etc.

The patient was sent to the hospital for **observation.**

It was agreed that the plan should be submitted to the committee for their **observation.**

The council insists upon the **observance** of the Sabbath.

councilor   A member of a council or assembly.
counselor   An advisor; a lawyer.

Councilor Jones did not like the manner in which the city **counselor** handled the legal situation.

bullion   Uncoined gold or silver.
bouillon   A clear broth or soup.

(These definitions are self-evident; the pronunciations are **bullion: buhl'yun; bouillon: boo'yahn,** or **buhl'yun.**)

carton   A box made of pasteboard.
cartoon   An amusing drawing of persons or things.

(**Carton** is accented on the first syllable: **car'ton,** but **cartoon** is accented on the last syllable: **cartoon'.**)

27

Adjectives

Study the definitions of the following adjectives so that you will be able to recast the sentences in the next lesson as requested.

candid	Truthful; frank; not prejudiced.
legible	Capable of being read; plain.
graphic	Vivid; lifelike; clearly expressed.
belated	Delayed beyond the usual or expected time.
audible	Capable of being heard.
latent	Hidden; not visible or apparent.
furtive	Sly; stealthy; thief-like.
flexible	Not rigid; pliable; easily bent.
available	Ready for use; handy.
indulgent	Lenient; inclined to give way to; tolerant.
benevolent	Charitable; desiring to do good for others.
pertinent	Pertaining to; relating to.

Exercise

1. What is the noun form of **candid**?
2. Give an antonym for **latent**.
3. Construct a sentence with the verb form of **indulgent**.
4. Write two phrases that will contain **audible**; **graphic**.
5. What is the meaning of **impertinent to the subject**?
6. When is one's writing **illegible**?

28

Review of Adjectives

Recasting Exercise

Rewrite the following sentences by using a word from the preceding list, retaining the original meaning of the sentence:

1. Funds may now be obtained for the new municipal building.
2. What he had to say had nothing to do with the study of history.
3. One could easily read his handwriting.
4. The rule is so worded as to permit of other interpretations.
5. Voices could be heard coming from the basement.
6. The reporter gave a very clear account of the accident.

7. We hope you will excuse this overdue report.

8. He looked at me in a very sly way.

9. Their enmity toward our country, although it is not evident, is still there.

10. Give me your honest opinion of his work.

11. His parents are altogether too kind and easy with him.

12. He possessed a spirit that made him willing to help other people.

Completion Drill

Fill each blank to complete the meaning of the sentence:

1. **Benevolent** is accented on the _____ syllable.

2. The antonym for **pertinent** is _____.

3. **Audible** is derived from the Latin _____ which means _____.

4. The noun form of **legible** is _____.

5. Two synonyms for **inflexible,** when reference is made to an officer or ruler, are _____ and _____.

6. **Graphic** is derived from the Greek _____ which means _____.

7. A **belated** answer or message is one that _____.

29

Two Troublesome Verbs

LIE AND *LAY*

These two words, though small in size, cause considerable trouble not only to students but also to professional people. This difficulty may be lessened or removed if the following plan, which has been successfully tried in various classes and vocabulary groups, will be adopted. Its significant feature is to substitute the meaning of the word to be used before deciding on the correct form, **lie** and **lay.**

I. Study the principal parts of each verb:

[44]

Pres. Tense	Past Tense	Pres. Participle	Past Participle
lie	lay	lying	lain
lay	laid	laying	laid

II. In your drills or exercises, first substitute the meaning of "recline" for **lie**, and "place" for **lay**.

Thus, suppose you were asked to fill each of the following blanks with the correct form of **lie** or **lay**:

a. He _____ his hat on the chair before he sat down to dinner.

b. Yesterday, I _____ on the couch for three hours.

c. The dog has _____ on that chair all afternoon.

d. Her books _____ on her desk during the entire vacation.

III. *Procedure:* The student should proceed mentally in this manner:

a. He (placed) his hat on the chair before he sat down to dinner.

b. Yesterday, I (reclined) on the couch for three hours.

c. The dog has (reclined) on that chair all afternoon.

d. Her books (reclined) on her desk during the entire vacation.

IV. *Check:*

In sentence **a** you will seek the past tense of the verb **lay**, which means "placed." It will be **laid**.

In sentence **b** you will find the past tense of the verb **lie**, which means "recline." It will be **lay**.

In sentence **c**, the past participle of the verb **lie**, which means "recline," will be used. It will be **lain**.

In sentence **d** the past tense of the verb **lie**, which means "recline," will be used. It will be **lay**.

(A surprisingly great number of people think or have been taught that the verb **lie** cannot be used in relation to inanimate or lifeless objects. This is incorrect. If the meaning is "recline," the verb will be some part of **lie** regardless of what the subject is.)

Drill

Fill each blank in the following sentences with the proper form of **lie** or **lay**. On a separate sheet of paper, first write in the parentheses at the end of each sentence the meaning or definition to be used, and then select the proper form of **lie** or **lay.**

Example:

The sick child _____ on the sofa until the doctor arrived. (   )

The sick child _____ on the sofa until the doctor arrived. (reclined)

The sick child **lay** on the sofa until the doctor arrived.

1. Kindly _____ this book on my desk. (   )
2. It will _____ there unless you pick it up. (   )
3. The child would not _____ down for his mother. (   )
4. Your coat is _____ on the floor. (   )
5. The cat has _____ there all morning. (   )
6. Who _____ that wet dish on the tablecloth? (   )
7. The command was, "_____ down, Spot!" (   )
8. I was asked to _____ a pencil on each desk. (   )
9. She thinks she will _____ down for an hour. (   )
10. Do not let those papers _____ on the floor. (   )
11. Now _____ my hat where it _____ before. (   ), (   )
12. Dad found his pipe _____ in the grass where it had _____ all night. (   ), (   )
13. Nervous people find it difficult to _____ still for any length of time. (   )
14. When the garden is properly _____ out, we shall begin to plant. (   )
15. The culprit was _____ a bomb under the porch when he was arrested by the police. (   )
16. Stretch the carpet so that it will _____ more smoothly. (   )
17. Mary _____ down this morning because she was ill.

(The frequent misuse of **lie** and **lay** justifies this careful and methodic study and plan.)

30

Achievement-Test Words

I. Multiple-Choice Exercise

In each of the following sentences, select the word or expression that best completes the statement. The boldface words have been taken from achievement tests. Consult your dictionary for the correct answers.

1. A **talisman** might be considered useful to:
   (a) bring you luck, (b) sell articles, (c) tell stories.
2. If you met a **gourmand,** he very likely would be:
   (a) an expert in testing food, (b) a hearty eater, (c) one who believes in many marriages.
3. If you were **opulent,** you would be:
   (a) very heavy, (b) extremely influential, (c) wealthy.
4. If you were considered a **misanthrope,** you would be:
   (a) a public benefactor, (b) a hater of mankind, (c) a lover of flowers.
5. Men of **arrogance** are:
   (a) disliked because of their haughtiness, (b) popular because of their influence, (c) in demand because of their speaking ability.
6. A **polyglot** is:
   (a) a geometric figure having many sides, (b) an excessive eater, (c) a person who understands many languages.
7. If a new **parapet** is needed, reference is made to:
   (a) a piece of furniture, (b) a low wall at the edge of a roof, (c) a mosaic floor.
8. No doubt you do not like a **harangue** because it is:
   (a) not your favorite pie, (b) too noisy and ranting, (c) requires much space.
9. If you are seeking a **panacea,** you are looking for:
   (a) a cure-all, (b) a popular breakfast dish, (c) a high place with an unobstructed view.
10. You do not approve of **chicanery** because:
    (a) it is unfair practice, (b) it is weaker than coffee, (c) sometimes the jokes are offensive.

11. The youngster objected to a **modicum** of dessert because it was:

(*a*) too tart, (*b*) too small a portion, (*c*) not sweet enough.

12. A **pragmatic** person is one who:

(*a*) likes to dictate to others, (*b*) is not very active, {*c*} is concerned with practical results.

II. Exercise

1. How does **talisman** differ from **talesman?**
2. Why should one not **gormandize?**
3. What is the definition of **misanthropy?**

31

Word Origins

carnival

If the two words **carne** and **vale** were joined together, the result would be a word that would closely resemble our English word **carnival.** This Italian and Latin expression **carne vale** means "O flesh, farewell!" or "Good-bye meat!" It had reference to the Tuesday preceding Ash Wednesday, which is the first day of Lent. In the early times when the tempo of living was leisurely and peaceful, and not of the hurry-scurry type of today, the people rigorously followed the Lenten regulations pertaining to amusements, light eating, and abstinence. During the seven-week period meat was a comparative stranger to every table. Hence, it was the custom to celebrate the last pre-Lenten day by eating and merrymaking. Today one often hears of a carnival to which is given the name *Mardi Gras.* This is French for Fat Tuesday, the eve of Ash Wednesday, a day for feasting and merriment.

leech

The reader may be surprised to learn that the word for the bloodsucking worm was once applied to physicians. **Leech** is derived from the Anglo-Saxon **laece,** which means "healer."

[48]

Consequently, physicians who were healers were called **leeches.** Until a little over a century ago, leeches (the worms) were used to bleed patients. This was a common practice because the belief was that most ailments were due to an excess of blood. Gradually, the term was shifted from the physician to the worm.

bonfire

The word has a gruesome origin. In the days of the bow and arrow when fortifications were assaulted and battered by huge stones slung from a catapult (the great attacking machine of that period), the soldiers often could not find time to bury the dead. The corpses were piled high and burned. At one time, the burning of heretics at the stake was a common form of punishment. These pyres were called **bonefires, or** fires of bones. Later they came to mean huge fires for public celebrations, and the original spelling was happily changed to **bonfires.**

32

Vocabulary Game

IZE WORDS

Substitute a verb ending in **ize** or **ized** for the boldface expression in each of the following sentences. Retain the original meaning of the sentence. The first letter of the desired word is given at the end of the sentence.

1. Yale **suffered a loss** of five yards for offside play. **(P)**
2. The government has voted to **help finance** the farmers. **(S)**
3. The young girls **think that** the new cinema star **is just grand. (I)**
4. The doctor **burned** the wound that was caused by a dog's bite. **(C)**
5. I shall **give** you **permission** to do this work. **(A)**
6. Kindly **write a summary of** the story for me. **(E or S)**

[49]

7. He found it difficult to **mingle** with other people. **(F)**

8. The speaker seemed to **talk about everything in general and nothing in particular. (G)**

9. The teacher could not **instill any spirit into** the class. **(V)**

10. If you deliver that speech, you will **endanger** your position. **(J)**

11. He found it difficult to **accustom** himself to our way of living. **(A)**

12. The press **held** his work **up to ridicule. (S)**

13. Students should **make good use of** their leisure time. **(U)**

14. Wherever she went, she always seemed to **do most of** the talking. **(M)**

15. The autoist tried to **make as little as possible of** the accident. **(M)**

16. The youngster refused to **say he was sorry** for throwing an eraser in the classroom. **(A)**

17. The governor was **highly praised** for his splendid administration. **(E)**

18. Spending money so recklessly will **soon leave** him **a poor man. (P)**

19. Our football team **beat to pieces** last week's opponent. **(P)**

20. Washington's great services to this country have **given** him **lasting fame. (I)**

33

Clinching Test No. 3

I. Matching Exercise

What word found in a preceding lesson will apply to each definition in the following list? The first letter of the required word is given.

1. To spring back.   r_____

2. Hidden; not visible.   l_____

3. To give new life to.   r_____
4. Truthful; frank.   c_____
5. To change or alter.   m_____
6. Roomy.   c_____
7. Able to be seen or felt.   p_____
8. To correct.   r_____
9. Not rigid.   f_____
10. Capable of being heard.   a_____
11. Interested but not prejudiced.   d_____
12. Lenient; tolerant.   i_____

II. *ATE* VERBS

Fill each blank with a verb ending in **ate** or the past tense of such a verb to complete the meaning of the sentence. The verbs will be found in preceding lessons. The first letter of the required verb is given.

1. We hope that the injury to the baseball pitcher will not i_____ him for the World's Series.

2. He tried to h_____ me in the presence of my employer.

3. Too much work is bound to e_____ you.

4. He was e_____ of the charge of setting fire to the building.

5. The officer will surely r_____ the charge that he accepted graft.

6. The speaker seemed to c_____ the audience.

7. He always tried to d_____ the other members of the organization.

8. Flies c_____ food.

9. The employer informed the strikers that he would r_____ by closing his shop indefinitely.

III. Questions

1. Give the correct pronunciation of:

   amicable   hosiery   auxiliary   fricassee

2. Tell the difference between the words in each pair;

uninterested; disinterested   *counsellor; **councillor

---

* Also spelled **counselor**.
** Also spelled **councilor**.

34

Vocabulary Exercise

If the student learns the definitions of the following words, he will encounter no difficulty in answering the questions in the next lesson.

deride	To ridicule.	**expedient**	Advantageous.
obsolete	Worn out; no longer in use.	**ingenious**	Talented.
paucity	Fewness; small number.	**desultory**	Disconnected.
		scrutinize	To examine closely.
denounce	To express strong disapproval of.	**opinionated**	Obstinate in regard to one's own opinion.
onerous	Burdensome.		
dynamic	Energetic.		
		imperturbable	Calm; serene.

Exercise

1. Construct three phrases containing each of the following adjectives:

dynamic _____	onerous _____
dynamic _____	onerous _____
dynamic _____	onerous _____
ingenious _____	expedient _____
ingenious _____	expedient _____
ingenious _____	expedient _____

2. On what syllable is **desultory** accented?

3. Does the first syllable in **paucity** rhyme with **paw** or **pow**?

Tell Me Why

1. You should not use **obsolete** expressions.

2. You do not wish to be considered an **opinionated** person.

3. You should **denounce** any ism that is designed for the overthrow of your government.

4. You do not wish people to **deride** what you say.

5. You dislike listening to a **desultory** orator.

6. You consider the duties of the President of the United States **onerous.**

7. You would like to possess an **imperturbable** nature.

8. You agree that the books of every bank should be **scrutinized.**

9. You would be dissatisfied with a **paucity** of ideas.

10. You think that the possession of a good vocabulary will prove **expedient.**

11. You would like to be surrounded by **dynamic** companions.

12. You think Thomas A. Edison was an **ingenious** person.

Exercise

Consult your dictionary for the answers to the following:

1. What is meant by **derisive** remarks?

2. What is the adjectival form of **denounce?**

3. What is an **obsolescent** custom?

4. What is a synonym for **imperturbable?**

5. What is an **ingenious** answer?

6. What word beginning with the letter **p** is an antonym for **paucity?**

7. What is the noun form of **scrutinize?**

8. What is the origin of **dynamic?**

35

Root Words

From the root words in this lesson are evolved many words of the everyday variety. A knowledge of these root words will facilitate the use of the words that follow.

I. **credo** (*pres. tense*), **creditus** (*past part.*), "to believe" (Stem: **cred** or **credit**)

[53]

Substitution Exercise

credit	credence	incredible	discreditable
credible	discredit	creditably	
creditor	credulous	credentials	

Substitute the word from the above lists that best agrees with the boldface word or expression in each of the following sentences:

1. The police acted **in a praiseworthy way** in suppressing the riot.

2. He did not receive sufficient **praise** for his good work.

3. The story he told was **one that could be believed.**

4. **Those to whom Brown and Company owed money** met to arrange some form of settlement.

5. My brother was advised not to be so **quick to believe everything he heard.**

6. Half of his testimony was **disbelieved** by the jury.

7. The record of our baseball team with no victories was **not an enviable** one.

8. The work was accomplished with **almost unbelievable** speed.

9. His **references** were instrumental in procuring the position.

10. We placed no **belief** in his account of the accident.

36

Words Frequently Confused

Concentrate on the definitions of the words in the following pairs if you wish to avoid trouble with them in the future. Construct original sentences containing the various words in this lesson.

restive   Stubbornly resisting control or authority; unmanageable.

restless   Uneasy; unsettled.

The people became **restive** because of lack of food.

Children in school become **restless** if they are not kept busy.

(**Restive** implies resistance to authority; **restless** implies uneasiness.)

divers (*adj.*)	Various; sundry.
diverse	Unlike; different.

We met on **divers** occasions to discuss the housing situation.

There are **divers** ways of solving that problem.

Their opinions were of a **diverse** nature.

irreverent	Disrespectful, especially to what is sacred.
irrelevant	Not pertinent; not to the point; extraneous.

We should not use the Creator's name in an **irreverent** manner.

The judge stated that the testimony was **irrelevant** to the case and must be omitted.

(**Irrelevant** is pronounced ir rel'uh vunt, not ir rev'el unt.)

plaintiff	The complainant in a lawsuit.
plaintive	Sad; mournful.

The **plaintiff** accused the defendant of stealing his car.

The mother of the convicted boy made a **plaintive** plea for leniency.

The song had a **plaintive** air.

loath	Reluctant; averse.
loathe	To detest.

The boy was **loath** to leave his home.

Some people **loathe** the very thought of work.

We **loathe** the subversive doctrines of such people.

37

Achievement-Test Words

I. Matching Exercise

For each definition in Column 1 on the next page find in Column 2 the word it defines and write the number of the word in the blank preceding the definition.

[55]

Column 1		Column 2
1. _____	Eagerness; greediness.	1. bilge
2. _____	Harmful; carrying infection.	2.˙ vestige
3. _____	To wrinkle or crease.	3. furtive
4. _____	Very generous; extremely liberal.	4. avidity
5. _____	A thorough investigation.	5. rumple
6. _____	Harmful vapor; unpleasant odor.	6. ruthless
7. _____	A trace; visible sign.	7. immune
8. _____	Sly; secret; stealthy.	8. dilemma
9. _____	Bottom of a ship; bulging part of a barrel.	9. inquisition
10. _____	Cruel; showing no mercy.	10. effluvium
11. _____	Not susceptible, especially to a particular disease.	11. munificent
12. _____	Preference between two unsatisfactory choices.	12. pestilential

II. Completion Exercise

Fill each blank with a word from the preceding list to complete the meaning of the sentence.

1. There is not a _____ of truth in what he says.

2. The inoculation will render you _____ to diphtheria.

3. The youngster gave the dish of candy a _____ look.

4. He was extolled for his many _____ deeds.

5. The ever-spreading malaria was attributed to the _____. which came from the swamp.

6. The tyrant was _____ in his demands upon the con quered people.

7. He has already displayed an _____ for vocabulary work.

8. The little girl tried hard not to _____ her dress.

9. He realized he was in a _____, and as a result re frained from acting immediately.

38

Pronunciation

Some of the words in the following list are mispronounced by many students and adults. A careful study of them will pay satisfying dividends. Learn their definitions as well as their correct pronunciations.

1. orgy	Excessive indulgence in some activity; a drunken revel.
2. comely	Of pleasing appearance.
3. renege	Failure to follow suit; failure to keep a promise.
4. autopsy	Examination of a dead body to find the cause of death.
5. heinous	Extremely offensive; very wicked.
6. bestial	Brutal; vile; beastly.
7. zoology	Study of animal life.
8. depravity	Wickedness; corruption.
9. assimilate	To absorb; to make part of oneself.
10. marshmallow	Soft, spongy candy covered with powdered sugar.

1. orgy	or'jee, not or'ghee.
2. comely	kum'ly, not comb'ly.
3. renege	re neeg', not re nague'.
4. autopsy	au'topsy, not autop'sy.
5. heinous	hay'nus, not hee'nus.
6. bestial	best'yal, not beast'yal.
7. zoology	zoe ol'uh gy, not zoo ol'uh gy.
8. depravity	de prav'uh ty, not de prave'uh ty.
9. assimilate	uh sim'uh late, not uh sim'yew late.
10. marshmallow	marsh mal'oe, not marsh mel'o.

Exercise

Fill each blank with a word from the preceding list to complete the sentence.

1. A new course in _____ will be given next semester.
2. Does the body _____ food?

3. The Girl Scouts toasted some _____.

4. There was an _____ of spending after the war.

5. She was a tall person of _____ appearance.

6. The coroner performed an _____ on the victim of the assault.

7. The judge rebuked the culprits for their _____.

39

Words Confused

AFFECT AND *EFFECT*

These words are so frequently confused that it may be profitable to elaborate on their various phases. Of the two, **effect,** the verb, presents the greater obstacle. But this may be easily and quickly removed if the student will associate the word **accomplish** with **effect.** If he wishes to use the verb **effect** in a sentence, let him see whether he can substitute **accomplish** in its place: if he can, it is very probable that **effect** is the correct word. **Effect** suggests effort and work to procure the desired end or result. A few illustrations will clarify this statement.

We must endeavor to **effect** a treaty with that country.

The talk relative to immoderate smoking **effected** much good throughout the school.

The medicine **effected** a cure.

(In these three sentences, **accomplish** or **accomplished** can be substituted without impairing or changing the meaning. It may be well for the student to know that **effectuate** means to bring to pass, to accomplish, or to give effect to.)

affect   To influence; to assume; to pretend; to impress.

effect   To accomplish; to bring to pass.

Illustrations:

The story did not **affect** me as it did you.

The soldiers **effected** a bridgehead in Italy.

[58]

The storm did not **affect** our plans.

The death of the executive **affected** the whole state.

The lawyer used every legal device to **effectuate** the release
of his client.

Exercise

Select the proper term from the words found in the parentheses.

1. Attempts to **(affect, effect)** better communication serv·
ice proved useless.

2. The mother in the presence of her child **(affected,
effected)** courage during the electric storm.

3. Her sadness is only **(affected, effected)**.

4. The reprimand did not seem to **(affect, effect)** him.

5. The disabled plane **(affected, effected)** a safe landing.

6. The new manager has already **(affected, effected)**
many changes in the firm.

7. Her pronunciation of the broad a is not natural but only
(affected, effected).

8. The war greatly **(affected, effected)** his mode of living.

9. The robbers **(affected, effected)** an entrance to the
store through an open window.

10. In order to remain away from school, the youngster
(affected, effected) illness.

40

Vocabulary Drill

A knowledge of the words in the following list will be necessary in order to do justice to the quiz in this lesson.

adroit	Skillful; clever.
drastic	Extreme; rigorous; acting with force.
imminent	Threatening to happen immediately.
laudable	Worthy of being praised; commendable.
explicit	Distinctly stated; clearly expressed.
mandatory	Like a command or order; obligatory.

atrocious	Very wicked or cruel; savagely brutal.
arbitrary	Unreasonable; based on one's own notions.
circumvent	To get around; to gain advantage by deception.
rejuvenate	To make young or vigorous again.
imperative	Urgent; not to be avoided.
capitulate	To surrender on certain terms or conditions.

Exercise

Explain the meaning of each of the following sentences. It would then be well for the student to develop original sentences using the boldface words.

1. The riot was **adroitly** handled by the police.
2. Nine new airplanes are **imperatively** needed by the airline.
3. The captured soldiers were **atrociously** treated by the enemy.
4. The members of the staff were **arbitrarily** selected.
5. Clothing prices were **drastically** reduced during the sale.
6. He stated **explicitly** that he would not seek re-election.
7. His side of the argument was **laudably** expressed.

"You Tell Me" Quiz

Which word in the preceding list would you use:

1. To describe laws which are very severe?
2. To describe a revolution that will happen almost immediately?
3. To describe a leader who refuses to listen to anyone's counsel except his own?
4. To state that all members must be present in order to vote?
5. To convey the idea that an act was extremely cruel?
6. To say that help is absolutely urgent and necessary?
7. To describe a skillful use of words?
8. To convey the idea that the military leader was ready to surrender?
9. To describe instructions that are easily understood?
10. To describe an act that merits praise?
11. To convey the idea that one tried to answer the question not directly but in a roundabout way?

12. To state that the football team seemed to have gained new life?

Adjectival Drill

Make each of the following adjectives qualify three nouns. This type of drill will enable the student to realize the elasticity of meaning and use of adjectives.

drastic	_____	arbitrary	_____
drastic	_____	arbitrary	_____
drastic	_____	arbitrary	_____
laudable	_____	mandatory	_____
laudable	_____	mandatory	_____
laudable	_____	mandatory	_____

41

Synonyms and Antonyms

State which one of the three words in each numbered group is neither a synonym nor an antonym for the word in bold type. The student should look up in the dictionary words in this list that are not familiar to him.

1. **allay**	associate	mitigate	lessen
2. **diligent**	sedentary	inactive	industrious
3. **gigantic**	colossal	immense	fantastic
4. **frugal**	careless	extravagant	economical
5. **indolent**	fragrant	sluggish	sprightly
6. **ultimate**	eventual	final	mediate (*adj.*)
7. **adverse**	helpful	propitious	returning
8. **tragic**	mournful	ludicrous	dramatic
9. **animated**	torpid	dormant	lengthy
10. **insolent**	tractable	submissive	sleepy
11. **intrepid**	cowardly	dauntless	radiant
12. **infamy**	disgrace	glory	hunger
13. **satiate**	surfeit	sprinkle	restrict
14. **discerning**	shrewd	complaining	sagacious
15. **pastoral**	bucolic	rustic	holy

42

Word Origins

disaster

From the earliest times it was believed that the stars affected the minds and ways of men. The stars were blamed for the troubles of individuals and were given credit for their good fortune. The present-day expression, "He may thank his lucky stars," is a hand-me-down from this early belief. **Disaster** stems from the Latin **dis,** "away from," and **astrum,** "star." So, if the stars were against you, you were certain to meet with misfortune of some description.

janitor

Janus was a Roman diety who was provided with two faces, one in the usual place and the other at the back of his head. He was considered the doorkeeper, and with his double facial set-up could conveniently see those who entered the building and those who left it. Today, the **janitor** has the responsibility of keeping a building in proper condition. **Janus** was also looked upon as the god of beginnings. This is evidenced by the naming of the first month of the year, **January,** in his honor.

alarm

This word is adopted from the French **a l'arme!,** "a call to arms." Originally it was a summons to get ready for battle. It gradually broadened to designate a warning signal, such as a fire alarm. Presently, it has, for many people, an unpleasant denotation, namely, the call to arise or the arousal from sleep by the alarm clock.

calculate

The Latin word **calculi** means "pebbles." Long before the invention of adding machines or the art of writing, the ancients apparently did most of their counting and computing with the help of little stones. The name of one of our advanced branches of mathematics, **calculus,** is derived from this source.

IMMINENT

43

Review

Description Exercise

Explain your selection of each boldface word.

1. Would you describe an agitated group of workers **as restless** or **restive**?

2. Would a heavy rainfall **affect** or **effect** your picnic plans for that day?

3. Would you call a lazy boy **impudent** or **indolent**?

4. Would you say that a person who spends money too freely was **frugal** or **prodigal**?

5. Would directions that are easily understood be described as **explicit** or **implicit**?

6. Would you prefer to be looked upon as an **arbitrary** or **arbitrating** person?

Quiz

1. What is a **pastoral** scene?

2. Why should we have **drastic** traffic laws?

3. When is an issue **circumvented**?

4. What is a **furtive** glance?

5. What besides food can be **assimilated**?

6. When does a person find himself in a **dilemma**?

44

Clinching Test No. 4

I. Completion Exercise

Fill each blank with a word or expression that will complete the meaning of the sentence:

1. The first syllable in **heinous** should rhyme with _____ _____.
2. To **circumvent** a question is to _____.
3. The g in **orgy** is sounded like the letter _____.
4. **Autopsy** is accented on the _____ syllable.
5. **Explicit** instructions are those that are _____.
6. A person is **arbitrary** if he is _____.
7. An **animated** speaker is one who _____.
8. A storm is **imminent** if it is _____.
9. A person is **indolent** if he is _____.
10. You **loathe** that which you _____.

II. Matching Exercise

For each definition in Column 1, find in Column 2 the word it defines and write the number of the word in the blank preceding the definition.

	Column 1	Column 2
1.	_____ urgent	1. **loath**
2.	_____ to accomplish	2. **restive**
3.	_____ sly; stealthy	3. **ruthless**
4.	_____ energetic	4. **furtive**
5.	_____ reluctant	5. **dynamic**
6.	_____ not to the point	6. **imperative**
7.	_____ cruel; showing no mercy	7. **effect**
8.	_____ resisting authority	8. **irrelevant**

III. Completion Exercise

| drastic | tragic | immune |
| adverse | intrepid | mandatory |

Fill each blank with a word from the above list to complete the meaning of the sentence.

[64]

1. The author made _____ changes in his manuscript.
2. He was _____ to the disease.
3. To attend the meeting was _____ for every student.
4. Our flyers were _____ young men.
5. The two boys met a _____ death.
6. She took exception to the _____ criticism.

45

Vocabulary Exercise

The student should familiarize himself with the meanings of the words in this lesson and endeavor to incorporate them into his active vocabulary as soon as possible.

dogmatic	Overbearing; positive.	**puerile**	Childish; foolish.
rigorous	Very severe.	**contentious**	Quarrelsome.
dilatory	Not prompt.	**transitory**	Fleeting.
insidious	Deceitful.	**condemnatory**	Expressing disapproval of.
oblivious	Unmindful; forgetful.	**intemperate**	Lacking in self-control.
spurious	Not genuine.	**procrastinate**	To put off till later.

Completion Exercise

Fill each blank with a word from the above list to complete the meaning of the sentence:

1. The leader's _____ utterances were not popularly received.
2. Cancer is an _____ disease.
3. We have just experienced a _____ winter.
4. The conversation was so interesting that we were _____ of the lateness of the hour.
5. His _____ use of profanity was inexcusable.
6. Earthly pleasures at best are only _____.
7. The _____ policy of the country cost many lives in the early stages of the war.

[65]

8. The document proved to be a ＿＿＿＿＿ one, much to the grief of its owner.

46

Review of Adjectives

Tell Me Why

1. You would not like to be described as a **dogmatic** person.

2. You would not employ people who are **dilatory.**

3. You avoid **contentious** persons.

4. You should not **procrastinate.**

5. You would refuse **spurious** ten-dollar bills.

6. You dislike a **rigorous** climate.

7. You disapprove of being **intemperate.**

8. You should not be too absorbed in **transitory** pleasures.

9. You do not subscribe to acts that are **insidious** in nature.

10. You would use **condemnatory** remarks relative to traitorous activities.

11. You should not be **oblivious** of your responsibility to your country.

12. You should strive to refrain from making **puerile** statements.

47

Vocabulary

Multiple-Choice Exercise

State which of the three expressions best defines the bold-face word. Consult your dictionary for the correct answers.

1. Flaunted his vocabulary.

(1) increased, (2) paraded, (3) condemned.

2. An **infringement** of the rule.
   (1) interpretation, (2) change, (3) violation.
3. Caused by **malice.**
   (1) ill-will, (2) anger, (3) defeat.
4. **Evoked** condemnation.
   (1) escaped, (2) called forth, (3) sought.
5. A **perpetual** tribute.
   (1) merited, (2) significant, (3) lasting.
6. **Encroached** upon his rights.
   (1) deprived, (2) trespassed, (3) explained.
7. A **subservient** person.
   (1) submissive, (2) difficult to manage, (3) destitute.
8. **Hampered** judicial proceedings.
   (1) demanded, (2) obstructed, (3) postponed.
9. A **stipulated** policy.
   (1) unworkable, (2) curtailed, (3) specific.
10. A **restrictive** measure.
    (1) prohibitive, (2) limiting, **(3)** unnecessary.
11. Sought a **curtailment.**
    (1) reduction, (2) abandonment, (3) elimination.
12. Voted a **diversion** of funds.
    (1) increase, (2) turning aside, (3) distribution.

48

Pronunciation

SIMPLE WORDS

Inasmuch as the mispronunciation of a simple word will call
forth more adverse criticism than a mistake in a difficult one,
it may prove profitable to focus attention upon the following
cautions:

1. elm	This is always a word of one syllable.
2. err	Let it rhyme with **sir,** not **care.**
3. film	Never say **fil'um.**
4. factory	Sound the letter **o.**
5. really	Contains three syllables: **re'al ly.**

[67]

6. diamond	Be sure to sound the letter **a**.
7. hundred	Stress the **r**. Do not say **hun'derd**.
8. athletic	Three syllables. Keep away from **ath the-let'ic.**
9. eleven	The first letter is **e**, not **el**.
10. delivery	There are four syllables in this word.
11. bravery	Do not say **brave'ree**.
12. formerly	Attention must be given the **mer** syllable.
13. genuine	The last syllable rhymes with **win**, not **fine**.
14. professor	Note that the first syllable is **pro**, not **per**.
15. arithmetic	Do not clip the letter **a**.
16. practically	It is **prac'ti cal ly**.
17. similar	The letter that follows the **m** is **i**, not **u**.
18. orchestra	Accent the first and not the second syllable.
19. contradict	Say: **con'tra dict**, not **con'ter dict**.
20. recognize	The **g** is not silent: **rek'og nize**.
21. governor	Three syllables are necessary. It is not **guv'-ner.**

Exercise

Explain the meaning of each of the following sentences:

1. A feeling of confidence **permeated** the country.

2. His **impoverished** vocabulary proved a great barrier to his becoming head of the firm.

3. The book was **mutilated** by the child.

4. Her participation in school activities was **negligible**.

5. Such a **malicious** tongue was bound to incur much enmity.

6. The schedule failed to **function** satisfactorily.

49

Verbs Taken from Achievement Tests

I. Matching Exercise

For each definition in Column 1, find in Column 2 the word it defines and write the number of the word in the blank preceding the definition. To do justice to this assignment, it will be necessary to resort to the dictionary.

Column 1		*Column 2*
1. _____	To charge; to attribute.	1. **delete**
2. _____	To operate against; to have force against.	2. **distort**
3. _____	To make clear; to explain.	3. **cajole**
4. _____	To surround; to encircle.	4. **impute**
5. _____	To misrepresent; to twist out of shape.	5. **languish**
6. _____	To cancel; to erase.	6. **militate**
7. _____	To imprison; to confine.	7. **disparage**
8. _____	To coax; to persuade by flattery.	8. **exemplify**
9. _____	To belittle; to speak of slightingly.	9. **acquiesce**
10. _____	To show by example; to illustrate.	10. **encompass**
11. _____	To accept; to submit; to comply.	11. **elucidate**
12. _____	To droop; to lose strength; to pine away.	12. **incarcerate**

II. Substitution Exercise

Select a word from the above list that may be substituted for the boldface word or words in the following sentences. The past tense may be used.

1. Parts of my manuscript were **thrown out.**

2. Such abusive statements will **go hard** against your position.

3. The dictator absolutely refused to **submit** to our plan.

4. We shall try to **make clear** what we intend to do.

5. Vocabulary building **takes in** many phases of English.

6. One should be reluctant to **speak ill of** another person's reputation.

50

Vocabulary—"Un" Words

Completion Exercise

unabated	Continuing; not diminishing.
unabashed	Not embarrassed or ashamed.
unflagging	Continuing with vigor; not drooping.
unalloyed	Pure; unmixed.
unavoidable	Not preventable.
unvarnished	Plain; innocent.
unadvisedly	Rashly; indiscreetly.
unquestionably	Certainly; beyond doubt.
unintelligible	Not understandable.
uncompromising	Unyielding; firm.
unconscionable	Unreasonable; not guided by conscience.
unprecedented	Never done before.

Fill each blank with a word from the above list to complete the meaning of the sentence. Ability to use these words, which contain the prefix **un**, will add luster to your diction.

   1. His family seems to be enjoying _____ happiness.

   2. The storm continued with _____ fury.

   3. The witness told the _____ truth to the court.

   4. A study of conditions proved that the accident was _____.

   5. The young legislator _____ presented a plan that embittered his colleagues.

   6. The speaker was _____ when his memory failed him.

   7. The factory ceased operations because of the _____ demands of the workers.

   8. His success was attributed to his _____ ambition.

   9. Peace seemed far distant because of the _____ attitude of one of the representatives.

   10. The foreigner's English was _____.

   11. You will _____ fail if you do not devote more time to your studies.

   12. The extremely severe winter was _____.

[70]

51

Synonyms

Substitution Exercise

allure	quietude	vestige	transitory
allude	discourse	propensity	coalition
curtail	circulate	beneficent	subterfuge

From the above list select a synonym for each boldface word in the following sentences. Resort to the dictionary for the correct answers.

1. There was not a **sign** of truth in what he said.
2. The writer longed for the **stillness** of the country.
3. The victory was occasioned by the **union** of three political parties.
4. The department has been requested to **reduce** its spending for the rest of the year.
5. The professor delivered a **speech** on "The Importance of Words."
6. The legislators resorted to various **tricks** to accomplish their purpose.
7. During our conversation he did not **refer** to the incident of last week.
8. To the dangers that lay ahead he gave only a **fleeting** thought.
9. Mr. Brown was praised for his many **kind** acts.
10. Who **spread** the story that my brother was going to **retire**?
11. Most boys have an **inclination** for baseball playing.
12. The agent's smooth talk did not **entice** me into buying the car.

Facts Worth Knowing

1. **Beneficent** is accented on the second syllable: **benef'-icent.**
2. The verb-form for **coalition** is **coalesce.**
3. **Vestige** is derived from the Latin **vestigium,** which means *footprint.*

[71]

4. The noun **discourse** may be accented on the first or last syllable.

5. Proclivity and **penchant** are synonymous for **propensity.**

52

Word Origins

sabotage

The French for *wooden shoe* is **sabot.** In the early days of modern industry, long before the workers were affiliated with unions, and before boards of arbitration to which the workmen might present their grievances were established, the method of expressing dissatisfaction with working conditions was for the laborers to throw their shoes (**sabots**) into the machinery and thereby damage it. No doubt the student can now see the relationship between the acts of the disgruntled workers of years ago and the present-day meaning of **sabotage,** "the malicious destruction of an employer's property by workmen during labor disputes."

senate

That "life begins at forty" is by no means a twentieth-century doctrine. The Romans apparently subscribed to the belief in certain important fields of activity. It was their opinion that reasoning and mental ability were linked with age. The more mature a person was, provided, of course, that he were of sound mind, the better his intellect was. With this philosophy they practically decreed that their most important legislative body, the Roman Senate, should be composed of elderly men. The word **senate** is derived from the Latin **senex,** which means, "an old man."

pariah

If one is considered a despicable person, unfit to mingle with society, he is looked upon as a **pariah.** By obnoxious deeds he has alienated his friends and the esteem of the public, and is left to lead a solitary existence. **Pariah** signifies "a drum beater." The people in the lowest caste in India and Burma were assigned the duty of beating drums at public celebrations, to inform the populace that the drummers or "untouchables" were not to associate with them in any manner. These people were branded outcasts by accident of birth and could never elevate themselves to a higher level. The present-day definition of **pariah** is "a social outcast, one despised by society."

53

Vocabulary Game

I. WORDS ENDING IN *IATE*

Recast the following sentences, incorporating a word that ends in **iate**. These are humorously called "meal" words, that is, "I ate" words. The past tense of a verb may be used if necessary. The first letters of the required words are found at the conclusion of the game. They are not presented in the order of the sentences. Focus attention on the boldface words for a cue to the desired word.

1. John will **act as referee** at the Yale-Harvard game.

2. The speaker seemed to **drift away from the main subject** in his talk.

3. He could find no one to **back up** his statement.

4. How long have you been **connected** with that firm?

5. The city is trying to **improve** the wretched living conditions of the poor.

6. That American has **renounced his citizenship and now votes in England.**

7. The mere mention of the defeat **made his blood boil with indignation.**

8. The child **made** his parents **miserable** in the presence of their guests.

9. We **turned down** their offer of assistance.

[73]

10. How do you **tell the difference** between the meaning of the words *ingenious* and *ingenuous?*

11. He said he would **pay Jones back** for the wrong committed.

12. The property in that neighborhood is beginning to **drop in value.**

13. The employer could not **win over** the employees **on** strike.

(First letters are: a, a, d, d, d, c, o, s, e, i, h, r, r.)

54

Clinching Test No. 5

I. Selection Exercise

puerile	rigorous	spurious	subservient
insidious	dilatory	transitory	disparaging
distorted	alluring	unprecedented	unintelligible

What adjective from the above list would you use to describe:

1. Money that is counterfeited?
2. A story that has been misrepresented?
3. A very severe winter?
4. A statement intended to belittle a person or deed?
5. A tempting offer for your property?
6. Pleasures that are fleeting?
7. Business gains greater than any made in the past?
8. A foolish or childish argument?
9. A person who is not prompt?
10. English that cannot be understood?
11. A follower who is very submissive?
12. A treacherous plot?

II. Substitution Exercise

evoke	quietude	circulate	intemperate
delete	oblivious	propensity	elucidate
hamper	stipulate	encompass	subterfuge

In each of the following sentences substitute a word from the preceding list for the boldface word or expression that will retain the meaning of the sentence. The past tense of a verb may be used.

1. My son has shown no **inclination** for school-teaching.
2. His illness was only an **excuse** to remain away from school.
3. They are beginning to **spread** stories that you will soon retire.
4. You did not **specify** what the monthly payments should be.
5. Father was **unmindful** of the lateness of the hour.
6. He is an **incessant** cigarette smoker.
7. Let me **explain** the meaning of this formula.
8. The student sought the **stillness** of the library.
9. It was necessary to **wipe out** twenty pages of the manuscript.
10. The child's impudence **filled** me **with** anger.
11. This project will **take in** several areas.
12. Too many outside activities **hindered** her progress in school.

55

Vocabulary Drill

Study the definitions of the following words preparatory to doing the exercise in the next lesson.

attest	To give proof of; to affirm to be true.
decry	To condemn; to make little of.
coerce	To compel; to force.
caption	The heading of a chapter or page; title.
permeate	To spread through; to penetrate.
obdurate	Stubborn; unyielding; hard-hearted.
palliate	To ease without curing; to mitigate.
visualize	To form a mental picture of.

abeyance	Temporary inactivity or suspension.
subjugate	To conquer; to subdue; to overcome.
abominable	Disgusting; unpleasant; hateful.
crystallize	To assume a fixed and definite form.

Exercise

1. Construct original sentences with:

coercive measures	**visual education**
abominable plan	**attestation of loyalty**

2. Explain the following:

an obdurate judge	subjugation of fear
the plans crystallized	**palliation of the offense**

3. Write the noun forms of: **coerce; subjugate, abominable.**

Completion Drill

Fill each blank with a word taken from the preceding list to complete the meaning of the sentence. Some words are used twice. The past tense of a verb may be used if necessary.

1. When spelling a difficult word, one should just try to _____ it.

2. The medicine seemed to _____ the pain.

3. Public interest in schools is beginning to _____.

4. He was severely criticized for his _____ act.

5. The names of the winners were kept in _____ for one week.

6. They tried to _____ employees to contribute to the campaign fund.

7. His confession failed to _____ the crime.

8. There was no necessity for using such _____ language.

9. It would be advisable to change the _____ of your story.

10. Did the expert _____ to the genuineness of the document?

11. The leader was _____ in his demands for higher wages for the men.

12. We knew the government would _____ the use of force.

13. The dictator's plan was to _____ the people of the adjacent countries.

14. A feeling of unrest seems to _____ the country.

15. Belief that he committed the crime is beginning to _____ .

16. The odor of paint _____ the auditorium.

17. The use of slang is _____ by all teachers of English.

18. The successful football season _____ to the splendid type of coaching the team received.

56

Words Frequently Confused

In this lesson you will find in each group, not two, but three words which present occasional difficulty to the student. This may necessitate more careful study, but the effort will be worth while.

credible   Able to be believed.
credulous   Inclined to believe almost anything.
creditable   Respectable; suitable; worthy of praise.

Few fishermen tell **credible** stories of what they caught.
Sometimes our people unfortunately are too **credulous**.
He performed **creditable** work while employed by us.
Our basketball team made a **creditable** showing against the leading college teams in the country.

respectful   Full of respect; showing consideration.
respectable   Worthy of respect; fair in size or quantity.
respective   Relating to particular persons or things, each to each.

1. We should always be **respectful** of the rights of others.
2. All children should be taught **respectful** manners.
3. He belongs to a **respectable** family.
4. Our baseball team won by a **respectable** score.
5. The boys went to their **respective** homes immediately after the meeting.

[77]

6. Smith, Jones, and Brown receive salaries of $5,000, $7,000, and $9,000 **respectively.**

missal	A book containing prayers for every day of the year; a prayerbook.
missile	An object that is thrown or shot, as a stone or bullet.
missive	A letter; a written message.

He never forgets to take his **missal** to church.

A **missile** came through one of the windows during a lecture hour.

The **missive** was delivered to the mayor by my secretary.

oculist	One who specializes in diseases of the eye.
optician	One who makes and deals in eyeglasses, lenses, and so forth.
optometrist	One who examines the eyes for the purpose of fitting glasses and prescribes for glasses.

(The definitions need no explanation.)

57

Pronunciation

Pronounce the words in the following list and then check your pronunciation with the forms given below. If the number correct is seven, you may feel justifiably proud. Also learn the meanings of the ten words.

1. **acme**	Top; highest point.
2. **façade**	The face of a building.
3. **impious**	Wicked; wanting in religious reverence.
4. **casualty**	Injury or death from an accident; a mishap.
5. **poignant**	Touching; keen.
6. **ricochet**	The rebounding of anything along the ground or water.
7. **askance**	With a side glance; hence, with suspicion.
8. **condolence**	Expression of sympathy with one in sorrow.

9. indictment   A formal accusation.
10. accompanist   One who plays an instrument, usually for a singer.

Check Your Answers

1.	acme	ak'me, not ak'uh me
2.	façade	fuh sahd', not fuh sayed'
3.	impious	im'pee us, not im pye'us
4.	casualty	kaz'u ul ty, not kas u al'uh ty
5.	poignant	poin'yunt or poin'unt, not poig'nunt
6.	ricochet	rik uh shay', not rik uh shet'
7.	askance	uh skanse', not ask'unse
8.	condolence	kon doe'lense, not kon'doe lense
9.	indictment	in dyt'ment, not in dikt'ment
10.	accompanist	uh kum'puh nist, not uh kum'puh ne ist

Exercise

Fill each blank with a word from the above list to complete the meaning of the sentence. Read the finished sentence aloud.

1. A letter of _____ was sent to the parents of the deceased student.

2. If you waste your time now in school or college, you will have _____ regrets later in life.

3. He seems to have reached the _____ of success in his profession.

4. We looked _____ at the professor when he said we would have to attend class on the holiday.

5. The charge that our students were improperly prepared was an _____ of the faculty.

58

Achievement-Test Words

What Is Your Answer?

1. If you felt **jaded,** would you feel:
   (1) ill, (2) tired from severe tasks, (3) angry?

[79]

2. If something is **integrated**, is it:
  (1) made a part of the whole plan, (2) discarded, (3) broken up?

3. If progress is **impeded**, does it mean that it is:
  (1) encouraged, (2) obstructed, (3) removed?

4. If a person is accused of being **mendacious**, does it mean that he is:
  (1) a heavy eater, (2) a thief, (3) given to lying?

5. If a problem has many **intricacies**, does it mean that it:
  (1) can be easily solved, (2) has many fine points, (3) is complicated?

6. If you met a **hedonist**, would he be:
  (1) a pleasure-lover, (2) a woman-hater, (3) a head-strong person?

7. If you told **lugubrious** stories, would they be:
  (1) terrifying, (2) sad, (3) profound?

8. If your plans are **inchoate**, are they:
  (1) incomplete, (2) not satisfactory, (3) impractical?

9. If difficulties are **obviated**, are they:
  (1) placed in the way, (2) made worse, (3) removed?

10. If a person is **benignant**, is he:
  (1) sickly, (2) miserly, (3) kind?

11. If **coercive** measures are employed, does it mean they are:
  (1) compulsory, (2) helpful, (3) sought for?

12. If a statement is **clarified**, is it one that is:
  (1) expressed, (2) explained, (3) made obscure?

13. If you are in **destitute** circumstances, does it mean that you are:
  (1) poor, (2) unhappy, (3) old?

14. If a person tries to **circumvent** an order, does it mean that he attempts:
  (1) to issue one, (2) to get around one, (3) to change one?

Cautions

1. The first syllable of **hedonist** is **he** and rhymes with **key**.
2. **Intricacies** is accented on the first syllable.
3. **Inchoate** has two recorded pronunciations.
4. **Lugubrious** is pronounced **lew gew′bre us**.

59

Word Origins

pedagogue

The ancient Greeks, especially those of the wealthy class, kept a large retinue of slaves. Among the latter would be singled out one who had manifested qualities of honesty, obedience, and intelligence. To this person was entrusted the care of the master's children. He would escort them to and from school and would supervise their recreational activities. Eventually, he was assigned to help the youngsters with their lessons, thus serving as their tutor. From this meaning was evolved the present-day acceptance of the word, namely, "a teacher or schoolmaster." **Pedagogue** is derived from the Greek **pais,** "boy," and **ago,** "to lead." The first syllable **ped** is not related to the Latin **pes, pedis,** which means "foot."

X ray (n.)

When Roentgen discovered the method of photographing the body internally, he did not know the nature of the waves that produced this phenomenon. Being mathematically inclined, he resorted to the sphere of algebra for a suitable term and decided on the letter **x,** the algebraic symbol for the unknown quantity. Thus analyzed, it means "the unknown ray."

recalcitrant

When we speak of a **recalcitrant** person, we think of one who is disobedient, rebellious, and faultfinding. To get the real force of this word, we must go to its origin or etymology. A **recalcitrant** person is one who is a "kicker"; that is, very stubborn and obstinate. This word is derived from the Latin **re,** "back," and **calcitare,** "to kick." In other words, he shows his heels **(calces),** not in running, but in the type of kicking that is used by an unruly or ungovernable mule.

pantry

A **pantry** is not a place to store pans. It comes from the Latin **panis,** "bread," hence, the room where bread was kept.

60

Review

The boldface words are found in previous lessons.

Quiz

1. Why is a **dogmatic** person usually disliked?
2. Would you describe the climate of California or Florida as **rigorous**?
3. When is a person **coerced** into doing something?
4. When does one speak **unintelligibly**?
5. Why should we refrain from making **disparaging** remarks?
6. What is a **creditable** high school record for a student?
7. Does the second syllable of **indictment** rhyme with **kite** or **kick**?
8. Would you call a stone a **missile** or **missive**?
9. What is **spurious** money?

$$9 \times 7 \times 7 = ?$$
$$7 \times 7 \times 9 = ?$$

PEDAGOGUE

Clinching Test No. 6

I. Multiple-Choice Exercise

Which one of the three words at the right best defines the boldface word in the expression at the left?

1. The **missive** was found.   (1) letter, (2) stone, (3) prayer-book.

2. An **obdurate** leader.   (1) flexible, (2) unyielding, (3) complaining.

3. Later **deposed**.   (1) presented, (2) rested, (3) put out.

4. Held in **abeyance**.   (1) danger, (2) prison, (3) suspension.

5. **Decried** the act.   (1) advocated, (2) condemned, (3) understood.

6. **Antecedent** events.   (1) previous, (2) later, (3) important.

7. Acted **diffidently**.   (1) quickly, (2) timidly, (3) ignorantly.

8. An **impious** act.   (1) sacred, (2) reverent, (3) wicked.

9. A **credulous** student.   (1) gullible, (2) indolent, (3) ambitious.

10. **Complacent** people.   (1) happy, (2) self-satisfied, (3) pleasing.

11. He looked **askance**.   (1) sideways, (2) thin, (3) bewildered.

12. A **poignant** thought   (1) warlike, (2) stimulating, (3) piercing.

What Is Your Answer?

Explain the meaning of each boldface word and then answer the question that is asked.

1. What is an **inchoate** plan?
2. When is a rule **circumvented**?
3. Do you enjoy **lugubrious** stories? Your reason?

4. Why does one usually dislike **recalcitrant** children?
5. What is a **clarified** remark?
6. What is a **hedonist**?
7. Why should you show **deference** to your superiors?
8. What is meant by "a **continent** nature"?
9. Why should you not wish to be called "**ruthless**"?
10. When is a decision held in **abeyance**?
11. When are people **destitute**?

62

Vocabulary

Recasting Exercise

vibrate	To swing back and forth; to thrill.
augment	To make larger; to increase.
veracity	Truthfulness; correctness.
assertive	Positive; too confident.
relinquish	To let go; to give up.
anticipate	To expect; to look forward to.
terminate	To put an end to; to cease.
resumption	A beginning again after an interruption.
approximate	To come near to in amount, etc.; to approach closely.
precautionary	Using foresight or care beforehand.

Rewrite each of the following sentences, using a word from the above list that will retain the original meaning of the sentence. The past tense may be used if necessary.

1. Our house practically rocked whenever a heavy truck passed it.
2. He is known for never trying to juggle the truth.
3. Do you bank on going to New York next month?
4. We had better take a long look ahead before agreeing to his proposition.
5. He won't be with our firm after July 1.
6. He was unpopular because he thought he knew the answer to every problem.

7. Our factory will open next week after being closed for two months.

8. Pile up as many good vocabulary words as possible.

9. The cost of the house will come close to $10,000.

10. The dog would not let go of the boy's cap.

Quiz

1. What is the sound of the last syllable in **approximate** when used as an adjective?

2. Explain:

    (a) Her heart **vibrated** at the mere mention of vacation

    (b) Next Friday will be the **terminal** day for the essay contest.

    (c) We should strive for **word-augmentation.**

63

Vocabulary

ADJECTIVES

Learn the definitions of the adjectives in this lesson so that you will be able to use them in your daily speech and also to answer the questions relating to them which will appear in subsequent exercises.

tacit	Unspoken; implied but not stated outright.
ardent	Fiery; eager; very enthusiastic.
odious	Hateful; offensive; very displeasing.
abstruse	Hard to understand.
obvious	Easily seen or understood; plain; evident.
salient	Prominent; conspicuous.
radical	Extreme; deep-seated; fundamental.
cardinal	Principal; chief; fundamental.
mature	Full grown; carefully thought out; perfected.
caustic	Sarcastic; stinging; severe.
languid	Weak; lacking in energy; listless.
adequate	Sufficient; enough to meet a certain need.

64

Adjectival Phrases

Explain the meaning of the following phrases and place each phrase in an original sentence.

tacit approval	radical difference
ardent supporter	cardinal objective
odious propaganda	mature deliberation
abstruse explanation	caustic editorial
obvious goal	languid interest
salient weakness	adequate compensation

Exercise

Consult your dictionary for the answers to the following questions.

1. How does **abstruse** differ from **obtuse?**
2. What is the meaning of **obviate?**
3. How many syllables has the word **salient?**
4. Give the noun forms of: **mature; adequate; abstruse.**
5. Explain the meaning of: **tacit; taciturn.**
6. Write three phrases each of which contains the adjective **cardinal.**
7. From what language and word is **cardinal** derived?

65

Pronunciation

WORDS WITH NEW SECONDARY PRONUNCIATIONS

Pronunciation, like women's styles, undergoes occasional changes, but with a difference. In clothing, what was formerly in vogue is discarded almost completely; in pronunciation, the form once in vogue is always correct and invariably is preferred, but the word has received an additional pronunciation. *Webster's New Collegiate Dictionary,* which was released to the public in 1949, includes various new secondary forms, many of which will be presented in this book. The following words belong to that category.

clique

One is no longer obliged to make this word rhyme with **peak.** It is now permissible to let it rhyme with **pick.**

status

Although the dictionary-makers were unanimous in having the first syllable of **status** rhyme with **play,** you will not be accused of a mispronunciation if you make that syllable rhyme with **fat.**

scabies

Inasmuch as **rabies** always had two recorded pronunciations, the conclusion was that **scabies** likewise always had two pronunciations. This was not the case until 1949. It is well to remember that we cannot argue by comparison or analogy where pronunciation is the issue. Popular usage is the inflexible guide. Henceforth, students and all others may give three syllables or two syllables to **scabies,** that is, **skay'be eez** or **skay'beez.**

syringe

Whether this word is used as a noun or as a verb, you will not be restricted to accenting it on the first syllable. Accent the first syllable or the second and you will be correct.

The most effective way to familiarize oneself with the pronunciation of doubtful words is to incorporate them into sentences and then read the sentences aloud. In this way the ear becomes attuned to the correct form or forms.

Read aloud:

1. There are too many **cliques** in that organization.
2. His financial **status** is unquestionably satisfactory.
3. What is the **status** quo of Mr. Brown in his home town?
4. The **syringe** is in the medicine cabinet.
5. The doctor advised that the ear be **syringed.**
6. There is an epidemic of **scabies** in some of our schools.

66

Achievement-Test Words

I. Matching Exercise

For each definition in Column 1 below, find in Column 2 the word that matches it and place its number in the blank preceding the definition.

Column 1

1. _____ Elevated in rank, etc.; sublime.
2. _____ To produce as if by hatching.
3. _____ Radiant; shining brightly.
4. _____ Class; group with basic likenesses.
5. _____ Obedient; easily led.
6. _____ Odd notion; fantastic action.
7. _____ To meditate; to ponder; to chew again.
8. _____ Likely to arouse ill will; offensive.
9. _____ Whim; unreasonable notion.
10. _____ To make more certain; to confirm.
11. _____ To impair the quality of; to contaminate.
12. _____ Variation; change in circumstances.

Column 2

1. **genus**
2. **docile**
3. **vagary**
4. **exalted**
5. **caprice**
6. **vitiate**
7. **refulgent**
8. **incubate**
9. **ruminate**
10. **invidious**
11. **vicissitude**
12. **corroborate**

II. Completion Exercise

Fill each blank with a word from the preceding list that will complete the meaning of the sentence. The past tense of verbs and the plural of nouns may be used.

1. The lion and the tiger belong to the same _____.
2. He occupies an _____ place in that society.
3. We _____ on the events of the past year.

4. The cow is considered a _____ animal.

5. They desired to sit in the _____ sunshine.

6. Sometimes his acts are like the _____ of a dream.

7. My superior officer _____ what I said.

8. The air was _____ with cigarette smoke.

9. Allusion was made to the _____ of war.

10. We were tired of the _____ propaganda of the enemy.

11. Her refusal to dress formally for the dance was a mere _____.

12. The farmer will _____ a thousand eggs.

67

Root Words

Substitution Exercise

The words in this lesson will be more clearly understood and will require less memory effort if the student will associate their meanings with the roots from which they stem. The words in the following list should be made a part of the student's active vocabulary.

When the root word is a noun, the basic stem is customarily found by dropping the ending of the genitive or possessive case form. The word in this lesson is **caput,** whose genitive case is **capitis.** To obtain the basic stem, the ending **is** is dropped.

caput, capitis, "head"
(Stem: **capit, cap, capt,** or **cipit** (for sound).)

cape	A headland.	**decapitate**	To behead.
capital (*n.*)	The head city of a state; amount of wealth for a business.	**capitalize**	To make use of for profit.
		capitulate	To surrender under certain headings or conditions.
caption	The heading of a chapter or story.		
		precipitately	Hastily; rashly

precipice   A cliff; a steep, overhanging place.

precipitate To dash headlong; to hasten.

recapitulate To repeat, as the headings or chief topics.

Substitute a word from the above list that will convey the meaning of the boldface word or words in the following sentences.

1. The author has changed the **heading** of his story.

2. Such inflammatory talks may **quickly bring on** a war.

3. Marie Antoinette **had her head cut off** during the French Revolution.

4. The child fell from that **high, overhanging cliff.**

5. The soldiers were willing to **make terms of surrender** provided they could return to their homeland.

6. The football player tried to **make as much money as possible from** nis athletic ability.

7. We have a summer home on a **piece of land that projects into the sea.**

8. Brown & Company has $150,000 **to carry on its business.**

9. Some people try to **profit from** the mistakes of others.

10. After a discourse of one hour, the speaker **repeated briefly the main headings or parts of his speech.**

11. When he fell heir to a goodly sum of money, he **hastily** invested it in a rather doubtful invention.

68

Words Frequently Confused

After studying the definitions of the words in the following groups, try to construct original sentences containing the given words.

averse   Unwilling; opposed.

adverse   Acting against; antagonistic; calamitous.

Too many students are **averse** to hard work.

Father was **averse** to my driving the family automobile.

She cannot tolerate **adverse** criticism.

Smith's family found itself in **adverse** circumstances when he lost his position.

(**Averse** is used in regard to persons; **adverse,** in regard to things.)

momentous	Of very great importance.
momentary	Lasting for only a moment; done in an instant.

The President has to make many **momentous** decisions.

July 4, 1776 is a **momentous** date.

The child was in a **momentary** rage.

Pleasures of this life are at best only **momentary.**

elegy	Chiefly, a poem of sorrow for the dead.
eulogy	High praise, written or spoken, usually of a dead person.

(The definitions are self-explanatory.)

importune	To ask urgently and repeatedly; to trouble with demands.
opportune	Well-chosen; favorable; suitable.

The mayor was **importuned** by his relatives for political jobs.

The child **importuned** his parents for a bicycle.

We arrived at a most **opportune** moment.

cynosure	Center of attraction, interest, or attention.
sinecure	An easy and well-paying position with little work attached.

The football hero was the **cynosure** of all the girls at the college hop.

Too many persons are seeking **sinecures.**

The pronunciations of these words, which are found elsewhere in this book, are:

cynosure	sye'nuh shur, or sin nuh shoor
sinecure	sye'nuh cure, or sin'uh-cure

69

Word Origins

sanguinary

Which would the student prefer to possess, a **sanguinary** nature or a **sanguine** nature? Both words are evolved from the Latin **sanguis**, "blood." The former has the denotation of "being thirsty for blood; murderous"; the latter, of being "hopeful and confident." When a person's blood circulation is active and good, he is usually in fine physical condition and is inclined to be cheerful and hopeful, whereas one whose circulation is poor is likely to be sluggish and not very optimistic.

exorbitant

This word is derived from the Latin **ex**, "outside," and **orbs**, "circle." The student has often heard of the "day's golder orb," that is, the sun, and of the earth's orbit. Hence, when prices are out of proportion to value, or when **exorbitant** demands are made on an executive, they are outside the **circle** of what is considered right and reasonable.

delirious

When a person is **delirious**, his talk is often disconnected and meaningless. This word stems from the Latin **de**, "from," and **lira**, "track or furrow made by a plow." Therefore, one who is in a **delirium** is out of his mind or, colloquially speaking, "off the track of sanity."

exonerate

A person is **exonerated** of a crime or deed if he is freed from having had any connection with it. The burden of suspicion has been removed, thereby making him blameless and inculpable. The Latin **ex**, "from," and **onus**, "burden," make up this word.

70

Vocabulary Game

WORDS ENDING IN *CITY*

The English language abounds with words that terminate in **city**. Try to find those required for this game.

1. Beginning with **E,** this city stretches when pulled in opposite directions.

2. Beginning with **V,** this city is known to be truthful.

3. Beginning with **F,** this city is noted for happiness.

4. Beginning with **A,** this city is the home of boldness and daring.

5. Beginning with **P,** this city harbors smallness of number or quantity.

6. Beginning with **M,** this city is the opposite of truthfulness.

7. Beginning with **D,** this city is concerned with home and family life.

8. Beginning with **P,** this city likes to have its work known by all.

9. Beginning with **E,** this city contains that which is odd or peculiar.

10. Beginning with **E,** this city is the agent for light.

11. Beginning with **C,** this city houses partners in crime.

12. Beginning with **T,** this city believes in holding firmly to a purpose.

13. Beginning with **A,** this city holds only that which is genuine.

14. Beginning with **P,** this city refers to mental keenness.

15. Beginning with **V,** this city pertains to greediness in eating.

16. Beginning with **S,** this city is noted for its wisdom.

17. Beginning with **P,** this city is fond of fighting.

18. Beginning with **D,** this city is known for treachery and double dealing.

71

Clinching Test No. 7

I. Completion Exercise

averse	delirious	terminate	approximate
augment	relinquish	momentous	sinecure
assertive	capitalize	importune	precipitate

Fill each blank with a word from the above list to complete the meaning of the sentence. If necessary, the past tense of a verb may be used.

1. July 4th is a _____ date.
2. The parents were _____ to his buying a car.
3. He has accepted this extra work to _____ his weekly income.
4. His fiery and vehement talk almost _____ a riot.
5. The mother hopes to _____ on her daughter's acting ability.
6. The mayor was _____ by his followers to seek re-election.
7. That position is a political _____.
8. The patient became so _____, it was necessary to call a doctor.
9. His connection with the college will _____ in June.
10. The speaker began to be _____ when he felt that his power was weakening.
11. The number at the concert _____ two thousand.
12. He did his best to _____ his connection with the firm.

II. Matching Exercise

For each definition in Column 1, find in Column 2 the word that matches it and place its number in the blank preceding the definition.

Column 1	Column 2
1. _____ Offensive.	1. tacit
2. _____ Shining brightly.	2. docile
3. _____ Positive.	3. caption
4. _____ To look forward to.	4. mature
5. _____ Truthfulness.	5. abstruse
6. _____ To ponder.	6. cardinal
7. _____ Fundamental.	7. veracity
8. _____ A heading.	8. assertive
9. _____ Unspoken.	9. invidious
10. _____ Easily led.	10. ruminate
11. _____ Hard to understand.	11. anticipate
12. _____ Fully grown.	12. refulgent

72

Vocabulary

I. Matching Exercise

For each definition in Column 1, find in Column 2 the word that matches it and place its number in the blank.

Column 1	Column 2
1. _____ To banish.	1. deduce
2. _____ To praise.	2. deface
3. _____ To conclude from.	3. retrieve
4. _____ To destroy.	4. eulogize
5. _____ To mar or spoil.	5. inculcate
6. _____ To make dependent.	6. instigate
7. _____ To regain or make good.	7. ostracize
8. _____ To enroll, as in a college.	8. transport
9. _____ To incite or stir up.	9. subordinate
10. _____ To impress upon the mind.	10. demoralize
11. _____ To weaken in discipline or morals.	11. matriculate
12. _____ To carry from one place to another.	12. devastate

II. Completion Exercise

Fill each blank with a word from Column 2 to complete the meaning of the sentence. The past tense of a verb may be used if necessary.

1. The business man hopes to _____ his losses.
2. Children were asked not to _____ school property.
3. He failed to find a person who would _____ him home.
4. Who _____ all this trouble?
5. He was always willing to _____ his own interests to those of his country.
6. Lack of food and ammunition will surely _____ the troops.
7. What did you _____ from his remarks?

73

Vocabulary Quiz

I

This lesson pertains to the words listed in the preceding lesson. What word would you use:

1. To imply that someone was driven out of the organization?
2. To state that the inscription on a very old headstone could not be read because of age?
3. To convey the idea that you failed to enroll in the college of your choice?
4. To praise the work of your teammates?
5. To refer to merchandise that was sent abroad?
6. To mean that you studied the facts and arrived at a conclusion?
7. To state that you hope to make amends for your mistake?
8. To describe a city that was visited by an atomic bomb?
9. To convey the thought that the present fast pace of living will have a bad effect upon our civilization?
10. To imply that the fiery speaker caused the trouble?

II. Completion Exercise

Fill each blank with a word from the preceding list to complete the meaning of the sentence.

1. The last syllable in **subordinate,** the verb, rhymes with _____; in the noun and adjective, it rhymes with _____.
2. The noun form of **deduce** is _____.
3. The first syllable **eu** in **eulogize** means _____.
4. Three verbs whose last syllable is **duce** are _____, _____, and _____.
5. **Transport** may be a verb or a _____.
6. To **inculcate** high ideals means to _____.
7. The noun form of **instigate** is _____.
8. A synonym for **ostracize** is _____.
9. Three words which contain the prefix **sub** are _____, _____, and _____.

74

Root Words

Words have the common characteristic of being hungry for attention, and such attention, if displayed by the student, will pay dividends. Although some words may seem long and others may appear difficult, the student may, by using the scalpel—that is, by cutting them into parts—reduce the degree of difficulty to a minimum and give added interest to his word study.

I

pugnus, the fist   pugno, to fight
(Stem: **pugn** or **pug**)

Henceforth, whenever the student sees **pug** in a word, he may be certain that it refers to some type of fight.

Completion Exercise

impugn   pugnacity   repugnance
pugilist   repugnant   pugnacious

Fill each blank with one of the above words to complete the sentence:

1. If you are a prize fighter, you are called a _____.

2. If you possess a lazy nature, then work, as a rule, is _____ to you.

3. He was such an upright character that his motives were never _____.

4. If you are quick to argue or to fight, you have a _____ disposition.

5. If you have a strong dislike of the study of mathematics, then you have a _____ for it.

6. If you have an inclination to quarrel or to pick a fight, you may be rebuked for your _____.

II

rapio (*pres. tense*), **raptus** (*past part.*), to snatch
(Stem: **rap** or **rapt**)

Show the connection in meaning between the root word and each boldface word in the following sentences:

1. The student gave **rapt** attention to the talk on words.

2. The invaders obtained their food by **rapine**.

3. The **rapacious** attitude of some countries has been bitterly assailed.

4. She was **enraptured** at the thought of becoming a movie star.

5. The pirates of old were known for their **rapacity**.

6. The members of the football team were in a **rapturous** state as a result of winning the championship game.

Words Frequently Confused

Study the definitions of the following word groups until you are able to construct original sentences containing each word.

ingenious   Characterized by cleverness; shrewd; inventive.
ingenuous   Candid; frank; open; naïve.

He presented an **ingenious** plan for increasing production.
His speech was filled with **ingenious** remarks.
He was imposed upon because of his **ingenuous** nature.

(The pronunciation of **ingenious** is: **in jeen'yus**; of **ingenuous, in jen'yew us.**)

debar   To shut out; to hinder from enjoyment; to prohibit.
disbar   To expel from the legal profession.

A person's nationality or religion should not **debar** him from any organization.
He was **debarred** from the club for non-payment of dues.
The lawyer was **disbarred** for corrupt legal practice.

(Note that the prefix **dis** has three letters; the same number is also found in **law.** Hence, remember that **disbar** is associated only with **law.**)

illegible   Incapable of being read; not plain.
ineligible   Not qualified to be chosen; not suitable.

The inscription on the old tombstone was **illegible.**
Many signatures are **illegible.**
Failure to pass the examination made him **ineligible** for the position.

urban   Pertaining to the city or town.
urbane   Courteous; polite; refined.

The **urban** population is much greater than the rural population.
The secretary to the governor was an **urbane** and considerate young man.

76

Pronunciation

Read the following paragraph with your usual rate of speed:

For several days members of the maintenance department have been seen at the library. Years of neglect have left the building in a really disastrous condition. All the faucets are leaking; the columns are unstable. In fact, nothing seems to be in satisfactory shape. It was a grievous mistake not to have acted differently when requests for repairs and renovations were made. Perhaps the urgent appeal made last February by the executive board will see worthwhile action in the near future.

Through carelessness, students and adults often mispronounce simple words by omitting syllables. In the above paragraph are twelve simple words that deserve attention. Check your pronunciation of them with the following.

1. Did you give three syllables to **really**?

2. The second syllable of **maintenance** is **ten**, not **tain**. Say **main'ten ance**, not **main tain'ance**.

3. Do not say **li'berry**.

4. **Disastrous** does not have the letter **e** in it. Never pronounce it **dis as'ter ous**.

5. The first syllable in **faucet** is pronounced **faw**, not **fas**.

6. Do not put a **y** in **column**. Say **col'um**.

7. Did you pronounce the **o** in **satisfactory**? This word has five syllables.

8. There is only one **i** in **grievous**. Never say **gree'vee us**. It should be **greev'us**.

9. Be sure to sound the first **e** in **differently**.

10. Do not say **praps** for **per'haps**.

11. The first **r** in **February** is not silent.

12. Note that the letter that follows **c** in **executive** is **u**, not **a**.

77

Achievement-Test Words

Vocabulary Exercise

inert	Sluggish; inactive.
chasm	Deep opening in the earth; gap.
garish	Showy; gaudy.
callow	Inexperienced; immature.
brochure	Pamphlet.
captious	Faultfinding; difficult to please.
intrinsic	Belonging to the thing by its very nature.
egregious	Flagrant; conspicuous by bad quality.
extraneous	Not belonging; coming from outside.
inveterate	Deep-rooted; firmly established by age.
devitalize	To make lifeless; to weaken.
equanimity	Calmness; composure.

Selection Exercise

Which word in the preceding list would you use:

1. To describe colors that are glaring?
2. In reference to a person who smokes constantly?
3. In place of a small paper book?
4. To describe one who likes to complain?
5. To indicate that a great error had been made?
6. Pertaining to evidence that had no connection with the case?
7. In discussing the real value of a piece of jewelry?
8. In speaking about a gorge?
9. To convey the idea that youth is not experienced?
10. To state that a person has an even temper?
11. To say that very hot weather deprives you of your energy?
12. To describe one who dislikes to work?

78

Word Origins

anniversary

The completion or the turning of the year is often the occasion for a celebration. It is called an **anniversary,** and usually commemorates some important event. If the student will consult his dictionary for the etymology of this word, he will find that it is derived from the Latin **annus,** which means "year," and **verto, versus,** "turn." United, they form the "turn of the year." If a student were seventeen years old today, it would signify that he has been in existence for seventeen years, and that his eighteenth year has now begun.

tantalize

Tantalus was a character in Greek mythology. He was punished in the lower world by being placed in a body of water which reached to his chin, and by having suspended over his head heavily ladened branches of delicious fruits. When he would try to quench his thirst, the water would recede as he lowered his head; when he would endeavor to satisfy his hunger by eating some of the fruit, the branches would rise beyond his reach. It is from this dreadful punishment that the English language derives the word **tantalize,** which is defined "to tease by keeping something desirable in view but out of reach."

fiasco

A **fiasco,** according to the dictionary, is "a complete failure; a breakdown." It is said that the word originated from the slang of Venetian glass workers. If a piece of fine glass was discovered to have a flaw, or if a blunder was made in the operation, that piece was set aside and later blown into a flask. The Italian word **fiasco** means a "flask or bottle" which was produced, according to the story above, as the result of a mistake or failure. Such is the English signification of **fiasco.**

TERMINATE

79

Review

Select the proper form in the parentheses. The boldface words have appeared in previous lessons.

1. Because of his age John was (**illegible, ineligible**) to play on the basketball team.

2. Why are you (**adverse, averse**) to my going to New York?

3. As a rule five-year-old youngsters are (**ingenuous, ingenious**).

4. The (**importune, opportune**) arrival of the police prevented trouble.

5. The lawyer was (**debarred, disbarred**) from the golf club because of failure to pay his dues.

Explanation, Please!

Explain the meaning of each of the following sentences.

1. What did you **deduce** from the principal's remarks?

2. My brother is an **inveterate** smoker.

3. Who **instigated** the fight?

4. It is **obvious** he would be elected.

5. Loyalty to his friends was his **cardinal** characteristic.

6. His contract will **terminate** next month.

Clinching Test No. 8

I. Selection Exercise

disbar	rapacious	eulogize	ostracize
deface	ingenious	extraneous	retrieve
urbane	inert	matriculate	repugnant

What word from the above list might be used:

1. To indicate that one's lost fortune has been recovered?
2. To convey the idea that you have enrolled in a certain college?
3. To describe the effects of children's chalk-writing on buildings?
4. To state that a person has been excluded from society?
5. To describe a sluggish boy?
6. To imply that the remark did not pertain to the case?
7. To state that a lawyer has been removed from the practice of his profession?
8. To describe a very useful invention?
9. To refer to a plundering or grasping leader?
10. To praise the work done by your employees?
11. To describe a person who is polite and courteous?
12. To describe manners that are distasteful?

II. Completion Exercise

Fill each blank with a word or words to complete the meaning of the sentence. Explain the meaning of each boldface word.

1. Writing is **illegible** if it _____.
2. The **urban** population is found in the _____.
3. People are **demoralized** when _____.
4. A student has a **repugnance** for a subject if he _____.
5. One **subordinates** pleasure to work when he _____.
6. An **egregious** mistake is one that _____.
7. **Captious** people are always _____.

8. **Mature** judgment is that which _____.
9. A **garish** gown is one that _____.
10. News is **propagated** when it _____.
11. A **brochure** is _____.

81

Vocabulary

MULTIPLE USES

Read page 174 relative to the elasticity or many uses of words. The following exercise runs parallel to it. In your future study of words, do not content yourself with just one illustration. Try to form a number of sentences not only with the word assigned for the lesson, but also with its family members.

Terminate
"To put an end to; to limit or bound; to finish."

1. His contract with this company will **terminate** next month.
2. We thought his speech would never **terminate**.
3. All prayed that the trouble would soon **terminate**.
4. The story **terminated** in the marriage of the hero and the heroine.
5. We disliked the way in which the game **terminated**.

Termination. "End; conclusion."

1. At the **termination** of the meeting, we went to the theater.
2. The **termination** of the war seemed far off to parents whose sons were fighting.
3. Many unpopular measures were adopted before the **termination** of his rule.

Interminable. "Endless; exceptionally long."

1. He was an **interminable** speaker.
2. The delay at the railroad station seemed **interminable**.

Interminably (*adv.*)

1. They suffered **interminably** while in the prison camp.
2. He spoke **interminably** about his children.

Exercise

Construct original sentences with:

    terminal (*adj.* and *noun*)   **interminable**
    terminus   **termination**

82

Root Words

Some words undergo a change in spelling; others receive added pronunciations while the stems or root-meanings remain the same. The study of the roots of words will enable the student to view vocabulary-building in a different perspective and to retain the meanings longer than if he were to commit them to memory.

        anima, life; soul   **animus,** the mind
        (Stems: **anima** and **anim**)

animal	A living creature.	**equanimity**	Evenness of mind.
animate	To make active.		
inanimate	Lifeless.	**magnanimity**	Greatness of mind.
animation	Liveliness.		
unanimous	Of one mind.	**unanimity**	Agreement.

Completion Exercise

Fill each blank with a word or some form of a word found in the above list:

1. Man is a rational _____.

(He has a soul; he can reason.)

2. There was no _____ at the football game because the home team was being defeated.

(No pep or school spirit was displayed by the students.)

3. To show no hatred or dislike, but rather a spirit of helpfulness toward those who try to injure you, is an example of _____.

(Kindness instead of vindictiveness is practiced.)

4. Smith was chosen chairman by a _____ vote.

(All voted for him.)

5. A table is an _____ object.

(It has no life.)

6. There was an _____ discussion between the baseball umpire and the batsman.

(There was a rather vehement and heated exchange of words.)

7. To be kind to those who have spoken ill of you reveals a _____ spirit.

(A forgiving and noble spirit.)

8. He bore their insults and reproaches with _____.

(He was calm and serene and showed no desire to strike back at them.)

9. There was _____ among the members of the council that the young man's plan should be adopted.

(All were in perfect accord.)

83

Pronunciation

WORDS HAVING TWO PRONUNCIATIONS

Perhaps you have been in the company of educated persons and noticed that a certain word was pronounced differently from the way you were in the habit of pronouncing it. You might have been embarrassed and accused yourself of having mispronounced the word, when in reality the term in question had two recorded pronunciations. It might be well, therefore, to become familiar with as many words as possible that have two correct pronunciations. The following words have at least two correct forms.

[107]

1. debris	deh bree′	deb′ree
2. suave	swahve	swave
3. irate	eye′rate	eye rate′
4. apricot	ay′pre kot	ap′re kot
5. leisure	lee′zhure	lezh′ur
6. hygiene	hye′jeen	hye′je een
7. bouquet	boo kay′	bow kay′
8. ruffian	ruff′i un	ruff′yun
9. egotism	ee′go tizm	eg′o tizm
10. abdomen	abdoe′min	ab′doemen
11. gibberish	jib′erish	gib′erish
12. alternate (v.)	all′ternate	al′ternate
13. enervate	en′ervate	ener′vate
14. quinine	kwye′nine	kwuh neen′
15. penalize	pee′nalize	pen′alize
16. herculean	hercu′leun	herculee′un
17. tournament	toor′nament	ter′nament
18. irrefutable	irref′utable	irrefut′able
19. advertisement	adver′tisement	advertize′ment
20. appreciative	appree′shee ay′tiv	apree′shi a tiv

84

Vocabulary

PRACTICAL VERBS

Study the definitions of the following verbs before attempting to do the lessons that follow. Endeavor to make these words an integral part of your speaking vocabulary. This you can easily achieve through practice and repetitious use of the expressions.

avert	To turn away or aside; to avoid.
allege	To state positively; to assert without proof.
defer	To put off; to delay; to yield to the wishes of another.
infuse	To instill; to inspire; to pour in.
abhor	To shrink away from with horror; to hate.

conform	To act according to rule; to make like.
deviate	To turn aside, as from a course, way, rule, etc.
menace	To threaten; to direct a threat against.
pervade	To spread through; to pass through every part of.
emerge	To come out into view; to appear; to rise up.
submit	To yield; to offer as an opinion, request, etc.; to refer.
defame	To attack the good name of; to slander.

I. Drill

Fill each blank with the noun form of a word found in the preceding list:

1. The _____ was that the employer was dishonest.

2. One could detect a(n) _____ of confidence in his speech.

3. We should show _____ to the counsel and wishes of our parents.

4. Those people are a(n) _____ to any democratic country.

5. The charge that was brought against him was _____ of character.

6. There should be a(n) _____ between what we earn and what we spend.

7. He seems to have a(n) _____ for work.

II. Completion Drill

Select a word from the preceding list that will complete the meaning of each sentence:

1. The autoist tried to _____ the accident.

2. The secretary refused to _____ his resignation.

3. A feeling of optimism seems to _____ the country.

4. Our English teachers _____ the use of slang.

5. They will _____ action on this bill until next month.

6. Did he _____ that you stole his coat?

7. The students must _____ to the rules of this college.

8. The speaker seemed to _____ from his subject.

9. Many attempts have been made to _____ him.

10. That country has begun to _____ from its depression.

AVERT
85

Word Origins

maudlin

This is a corrupt form of **Magdalen,** who is often depicted with eyes that are red and swollen from weeping. Its present-day meaning has no association with the deep sorrow or repentance of Mary Magdalen, but rather with an emotional silliness usually caused by drinking. If the connotation of tears enters the picture, it is in the sense of "a crying jag."

companion

In the early centuries of our era, instead of speaking of "dining with" a friend, the expression used to convey the idea that you sat down and partook of a meal with a person was "to break bread with." Surely, if you thought enough of a person to dine with him, he could rightly be called your "friend or associate," the current meaning of this word. **Companion** is derived from the Latin **cum,** "with," and **panis,** "bread"; that is, "break bread with."

capital

The Latin word **caput** (genitive, **capitis**) means *head*. Many English words are derived from the stem **capit,** as is illustrated in a lesson on root words found elsewhere in this book.

The **head** is an important part of the body, notwithstanding the fact that a certain college professor stated that the only function that some students use it for is to prevent their collar or tie from slipping off the body. The **capital** of the state is the head or leading city. A **capital** crime is one of a serious nature, which in days long passed resulted in the separation of the head from the body: the criminal was **decapitated.**

procrastinate

A prescription for becoming a successful leader is, "Do not **procrastinate.**" If you have something important to do, try to do it at once, for, if you keep putting it off, you are said to **procrastinate.** This word originates in the Latin **pro,** "forward," and **crastinus,** "tomorrow." In other words, a **procrastinator** is one who puts off until tomorrow what should be done today. Let the student remember that a tomorrow never becomes a today.

86

Clinching Test No. 9

I. Why?

The student will explain the meaning of the boldface word in each statement and will answer the question that is asked:

1. Why does an audience dislike to listen to **interminable** speakers?

2. Why should young people **defer** to the counsel of their parents?

3. Why should **defamatory** language and writing be prohibited?

4. Why should we strive to **emerge** from shyness?

5. Why do our people **abhor** the thought of a totalitarian form of government?

6. Why do you think too much exercise is **enervating**?

7. Why would you object to being called an **inanimate** being?

II. Substitution Exercise

menaced	animation	conform
defame	terminable	abhorrence

Substitute a word from the above list for the boldface word or words in each sentence:

1. The contract is **capable of being broken** by either party.
2. His speech **threatened** the good name of our state.
3. The employer's acts did not **agree with** his promises.
4. She has a **strong dislike** for study.
5. The play seemed to lack **pep**.
6. Many people have tried to **slander** him.

87

Vocabulary Drill

A knowledge of the definitions of the following words will render the accompanying exercise easy:

turbid	Muddy; not clear.
sanguine	Hopeful; confident; ardent.
antidote	Something to prevent injurious effect; a remedy to counteract.
tenable	Capable of being held, maintained, or defended.
strident	Shrill; harsh-sounding; grating.
alleviate	To lighten the force of; to lessen.
responsive	Easily moved; ready to respond.
precarious	Not safe; dangerous; insecure.

somnolent	Sleepy; drowsy.
visionary	Dreamy; imaginative; impractical.
tractable	Easily managed; docile; easy to deal with.
recalcitrant	Disobedient; resisting authority.

I. Exercise

1. Name two adjectives from the preceding list that you would not like to have applied to yourself. Why?

2. What two words are antonyms?

3. If the audience generously applauds a speech or act, which word would describe such an effect?

4. Would you envy a person who has a **strident** voice? Your reason?

5. Which adjective is often used to describe a cow?

6. Use the antonym of **tenable** in a sentence.

II. What Is Your Answer?

1. If you were **tractable,** would you be:
(1) obstinate, (2) dull, (3) easily led?

2. If a child is **recalcitrant,** is he:
(1) sickly, (2) unruly, (3) shy?

3. If your troubles are **alleviated,** are they:
(1) lessened, (2) increased, (3) of a light nature?

4. If your friend has a **strident** voice, is it:
(1) soft, (2) very deep, (3) sharp?

5. If you were **somnolent,** would you be:
(1) wealthy, (2) hard to manage, (3) sleepy?

6. If you were an actor, would you desire to have an audience that was:
(1) somnolent, (2) visionary, (3) responsive?

7. If a plan or scheme is **feasible,** is it:
(1) practical, (2) real, (3) impractical?

8. If you saw the word **antidote,** would you say that it meant:
(1) a story, (2) a remedy, (3) a joke?

9. If a position is **tenable,** is it:
(1) easily captured, (2) capable of being defended, (3) in the process of construction?

10. If a stream is **turbid,** is it:
(1) muddy, (2) swollen, (3) flowing rapidly?

[113]

11. If you possess a **sanguine** disposition, is it one that is:
(1) cheerful, (2) sad, (3) timid?

12. If you have a **tentative** job, is it one that:
(1) pays well, (2) is experimental, (3) is dangerous?

88

Root Words

A knowledge of the Latin word which carries the denotation of "breaking" will pave the way to a more enlightened understanding of many words which the student has met but which he may never have associated with the root word.

> **frango** (*pres. tense*), **fractus** (*past part.*), to break
> (Stem: **frag, fring,** or **fract**) The letter **n** is dropped
> after the letter **a** to make the sound smoother.)

fragile	Easily broken.	**fragmentary**	Incomplete;
fracture (*v.*)	To break.		discon-
fraction	A part.		nected.
infringe	To trespass.	**irrefragable**	Not able to
infraction	A breaking		be broken
	of a rule.		or proved
refractory	Obstinate.		false.

I. Substitution Exercise

Select a word from the above list that may be substituted for the boldface word or words in each of the following sentences. The past tense of a verb may be used.

1. The **troublesome** boy was reprimanded by the principal.

2. He **broke** his arm when he fell from his horse.

3. We have received only an **incomplete** report of the trouble.

4. One should not **encroach** upon the rights of others.

5. Reckless driving is considered a **breaking of the law.**

6. In carrying that package, be very careful, because its contents are **easily broken.**

7. He devoted only a **very small part** of his time to the writing of his autobiography.

8. The statements made by the lawyer were **such that they could not be successfully contradicted.**

manus, the hand
(Stem: **manu**)

II. Exercise

If words derived from **manus** bear a relationship to "hand," let the student tell:

1. What is the nature of **manual** work?
2. What is an **amanuensis?**
3. What is the meaning of: "This boy would do better in some **manipulative** subject?"
4. What is a **manuscript?**
5. What are **manacles?**
6. What class of people have been **manumitted?**

89

Words Frequently Confused

A little study and concentration will enable you to distinguish between the meanings of the words in the following groups:

proscribe To condemn; to prohibit; to outlaw.
prescribe To order; to direct.

Their church **proscribes** dancing and cardplaying.
Free speech is **proscribed** in some countries.
We must do what the laws **prescribe.**

presentment A bringing forward or presenting.
presentiment A feeling that something is going to happen; a foreboding.

Presentment of the facts will take place at tomorrow's meeting.
He had a **presentiment** that he was going to lose his job.

[115]

callous   Hardened; unfeeling.

callow   Young and inexperienced; not fully developed.

The judge realized that he was dealing with a **callous** criminal.

The executive seemed to be **callous** to criticism.

The trouble was occasioned by a **callow** youth.

envious   Exhibiting envy; desiring to possess something belonging to another.

enviable   Arousing a desire to be like; desirable.

She was **envious** of her sister's golden hair.

She has an **envious** disposition.

Our football team has established an **enviable** record.

pretentious   Making claims to importance, worth, etc.; showy; ambitious in scope.

portentous   Threatening; foreshadowing evil.

The girls in the family are very **pretentious**.

A **pretentious** program was presented.

She had a **portentous** dream.

The President's talk seemed to have a **portentous** meaning.

90

Pronunciation

A study of the following words may be helpful in increasing your knowledge of their definitions and pronunciation:

1. **coup**   A brilliant, sudden stroke or move.
2. **schism**   A split or division.
3. **museum**   A building in which there are objects of interest in the arts and sciences.
4. **gaseous**   Having the nature of gas.
5. **derisive**   Expressing ridicule or scorn.
6. **hysteria**   Outbreak of wild emotionalism.
7. **ravenous**   Devouring; mad for food, etc.; extremely sharp.

[116]

8. desultory   Aimless; jumping from one thing to another without order.

9. chiropodist   One who treats ailments of the feet.

10. irrevocable   Incapable of being recalled or undone.

Check Your Pronunciation

1. coup   koo. Do not sound the letter **p**.

2. schism   sizm. Do not say **shizm** or **skizm**.

3. museum   mu zee'um. Do not accent the first syllable.

4. gaseous   gas'e us. Do not give it only two syllables: gash'us.

5. derisive   duh rye'siv. Do not make the second syllable rhyme with **hiss**.

6. hysteria   his teer' re uh. Do not say **his tair' e uh**.

7. ravenous   rav'in us. Do not have the first syllable rhyme with **brave**.

8. desultory   des'ul toe ry. Do not accent the second syllable.

9. chiropodist   kye rop'uh dist. Do not sound the first syllable **sher**.

10. irrevocable   ir rev'uh kuh b'l. Do not accent the third syllable.

91

Achievement-Test Words

What Is Your Answer?

exult   To rejoice greatly.

detest   To dislike very much; to hate.

apathy   Indifference; lack of feeling.

beguile   To mislead; to pass away time pleasantly.

decade   Period of ten years.

erudite   Learned; scholarly.

decadent   Growing worse; declining.

detraction   Act of belittling a person.

proclivity	A tendency; inclination.
ameliorate	To improve; make better.
calamitous	Disastrous; producing distress or misery.
incorrigible	Not yielding to correction.

What word, or a form of what word, from the above list would you use to improve the following sentences or expressions?

1. It happened more than ten years ago.
2. He seems to lean toward music.
3. A custom that is fast disappearing.
4. A youngster who pays attention to no advice and is difficult to manage.
5. The members of the team were mighty happy because of their fine record.
6. The members of his family are very well educated.
7. He cannot stand the thought of work.
8. We condemned the "I don't care" attitude of the public in regard to our school system.
9. They killed a few hours by going to the movies.
10. Rebuilding the slum area made living conditions much better.
11. There was no need for such knocking of his friend.
12. The father's loss of his job was tough for the family.

92

Adjectives

valid	Founded on truth; sound.
virile	Forceful; masterful.
turgid	Swollen; inflated.
facile	Fluent; acting with ease.
signal	Remarkable; out of the ordinary.
prolific	Productive; highly inventive.
trenchant	Cutting; keen; sharp.
repugnant	Distasteful; offensive; contradictory.

Explain the meaning of the following adjectival phrases and place each one in an original sentence:

valid argument	**turgid** stream
valid signature	**turgid** style
valid document	**turgid** utterance
virile leader	**facile** pen
virile achievement	**facile** imagination
virile opposition	**facile** tongue
signal honors	**prolific** writer
signal failure	**prolific** nature
signal victory	**prolific** brain
trenchant look	**repugnant** manner
trenchant editorial	**repugnant** work
trenchant criticism	**repugnant** characteristics

93

Word Origins

tawdry

This word is a corruption of **St. Audrey,** a city in England where a great annual fair was held. Laces and other articles which were sold here were of the type that may be seen at some present-day fairs: the laces usually did a disappearing or shrinking act after the first washing, and the other purchases were short-lived. Hence, the meaning **tawdry** came to be associated not with the place where the fair was held, but with the cheap and gaudy things that were displayed.

expedite

If your feet are tied, you are severely handicapped as far as speed is concerned. But if they are free, you can move rapidly. Use the scalpel on **expedite,** and you will find it to contain **ex,** "from," and **ped,** "foot," that is, "free-footed."

Impede, whose origin is **in,** "in," and **ped,** "foot," suggests having the feet tied and slow progress or hindrance.

salary

Salarium, a Latin word, means "salt." During World Wars I and II, sugar was a precious commodity and very difficult to procure. The soldiers were, however, given an ample supply of it. In the days of the Romans, salt was scarce, but the soldiers were considered so important that the small amount of this white substance **(salarium)** which could be obtained was given to them as part of their pay. Gradually, **salary** signified fixed wages, not of soldiers, but of employees in general.

dilapidated

If a student has a **dilapidated** vocabulary, he should seek the services of a good English tutor in order to strengthen it. An analysis of this word shows it to be derived from **di,** "from," and **lapis,** "stone," that is, stone falling from stone—in other words, a crumbling wall. It may be applied to anything that is beginning to decay or that has decayed.

RECALCITRANT

94

Review

avert	defame	menace
abhor	conform	submit

The above words are found in previous lessons.

Fill each blank with the adjectival form of one of these words to complete the meaning of the sentence.

1. The sight of a reptile is ——————— to her.
2. His work was not ——————— to the plans.
3. The police declared that the accident was not ———————.
4. The judge pointed a ——————— finger at the witness.
5. Who was the author of that ——————— letter?
6. Subjects of a dictator are ———————.

True or False

Which of these statements are false? Correct them.

1. The second syllable of **derisive** rhymes with **miss**.
2. **Interminable** speakers are very popular.
3. A successful writer usually possesses a **facile** pen.
4. Youth should **defer** to the wishes of the parents.
5. Public **apathy** can easily kill a worthwhile project.
6. A **trenchant** tongue is not an asset to any person.
7. The first syllable in **chiropodist** rhymes with **sigh**.

95

Clinching Test No. 10

I. SYNONYMS

turbid	erudite	precarious
strident	visionary	proclivity

Find among the following words two synonyms for each word in the above list. Do not use the same word twice.

shrill	insecure	unsettled	inclination
dreamy	tendency	intelligent	imaginative
muddy	scholarly	dangerous	harsh-sounding

II. Selection Exercise

State which one of the three words best defines the boldface word in each expression:

1. **Callow** youth.   (1) sickly, (2) hardened, (3) inexperienced.

2. **Tractable** people.   (1) good-looking, (2) easily managed, (3) downtrodden.

3. A **trenchant** statement.   (1) concise, (2) cutting, (3) accusing.

4. A feeling of **apathy**.   (1) indifference, (2) sadness, (3) dismay.

5. An effective **antidote**.   (1) story, (2) joke, (3) remedy.

6. A **ravenous** group.   (1) greedy, (2) angry, (3) stingy.

7. A **tenable** theory.   (1) vast, (2) defensible, (3) unpopular.

8. A **refractory** individual.   (1) injured, (2) retarded, (3) disobedient.

III. Pronunciation Exercise

Fill each blank with an appropriate word to complete the meaning of the sentence.

1. The second syllable of **derisive** should rhyme with _____.

2. **Schism** is pronounced as though it were spelled _____.
3. The **chi** in **chiropodist** is pronounced _____.
4. The letter **p** in **coup** is _____.
5. **Presentiment** is a word of _____ syllables.

96

Vocabulary—Everyday Words

A thorough study of the definitions of the following words will soon make them a part of your active, or speaking, vocabulary:

rustic	Plain; suitable for the country; unpolished.
sordid	Filthy; dirty; vile; meanly avaricious.
accrue	To be added; to come by way of increase.
repose	To rest; to trust; to sleep.
repel	To drive back; to reject; to force back.
affirm	To maintain as true; to declare; to assert strongly.
sustain	To keep going; to bear; to suffer, as an injury; to uphold.
imperil	To endanger; to bring into danger.
abolish	To do away with completely; to put an end to.
demolish	To pull down; to ruin; to destroy.
admonish	To warn of a fault; to scold gently but seriously.
engross	To occupy wholly; to take up all the attention of.

Substitution Drill

From the words in the preceding list, select the word which can best be substituted for each of the boldface words or word groups in the following sentences. The past tense of a verb may be used if necessary.

1. The voters have **placed** much confidence in their governor.
2. That tax will soon be **done away with.**
3. We admired their **simple and countrylike** surroundings.
4. In the spring, baseball seemed to **occupy all** his attention.
5. The state **suffered** a heavy loss in the death of the governor.
6. If you deliver that speech, it may **cost you** your position.
7. He is living in a **dirty and run-down** neighborhood.
8. Much benefit should **come** to you as a result of diligent vocabulary study.
9. They will start to **knock down** the old building next week.
10. He **declared solemnly** that he saw you talking with the prisoner.

11. The attack of the enemy was easily **driven back** by our forces.

12. His parent **scolded** him **gently** about keeping such late hours.

Selection Exercise

abolition	repellent	demolition
perilous	admonition	sustenance

Fill each blank with a word from the above list that will complete the meaning of the sentence:

1. The bomb caused the _____ of many buildings.

2. He was rebuked for his _____ table manners.

3. We contributed to the _____ of that poor family.

4. Youngsters should heed the _____ of their elders.

5. He was advised not to undertake such a _____ mission.

6. The speaker alluded to the _____ of the taxes.

97

Root Words

Many practical and worthwhile words are evolved from the root words presented in this lesson. The student should strive to integrate as many of them as possible into his active vocabulary. The dictionary should be consulted for the meanings of all doubtful words.

I. fundo (*pres. tense*), **fusus** (*past part.*), to pour out. (Stem: **fund** or **fus**)

fuse (*v.*),	to blend	**diffuse** (*adj.*),	wordy
infuse,	to instill	**fusion,**	a union
confuse,	to bewilder	**profusion,**	an abundance
refund (*v.*),	to restore	**transfusion,**	the act of
suffuse,	to spread over		transferring
diffuse (*v.*),	to scatter; to		from one to
	spread		another

Selection Exercise

Fill each blank with a word, or some form of a word, that is found in the preceding list to complete the meaning of each sentence:

1. If you are not satisfied with the purchase of this article, your money will be _____.
2. Copper and zinc are _____ to make brass.
3. This year's elections will see a _____ of three political parties.
4. The writer was too _____ to hold the attention.
5. A blush _____ the little girl's face.
6. Try to _____ into the minds of the students the importance of study.
7. The news of the disaster was quickly _____.
8. Many blood _____ were given to the victim of the automobile crash.
9. There was a _____ of flowers in his garden.
10. Every speaker should have at his ready command a _____ of adjectives.
11. Endeavor not to _____ the different words in this lesson.

II. grex, gregis (*gen.*), a flock.
(Stem: **greg**)

Exercise

Use in an original sentence each of the boldface words below:

1. If you like to be in the company of other people, you are **gregarious**.
2. If the boys are separated from the girls in the classrooms, they are **segregated**.
3. If a mistake or blunder is very conspicuous, it may be called an **egregious** error.
4. A group of people meeting for religious worship is called a **congregation**.
5. When people gather together, they are said to **congregate**.
6. If it is thought that a collection will **aggregate** $5,000, it means that such a sum is expected to be realized.

[125]

Achievement-Test Words

Multiple-Choice Exercise

Indicate by number the word or expression that will make the statement correct. Before attempting the answers, you should consult the dictionary for the definitions of the boldface words.

1. If your friend led an **ascetic** life, would it be one:
   (1) of pleasure-hunting, (2) of scientific study, (3) of self-denial?

2. If work is performed in a **perfunctory** way, does it signify that it has been done:
   (1) carefully, (2) neatly, (3) carelessly?

3. If you were **berated** by your employer, were you:
   (1) praised by him, (2) promoted, (3) scolded sharply?

4. If a word is **archaic**, should you in your writing or speech:
   (1) study it well, (2) discard it, (3) use it frequently?

5. If John is the **antithesis** of his brother, is he:
   (1) jealous of him, (2) similar to him, (3) the opposite of him?

6. If you were **nostalgic**, would you:
   (1) consult a doctor, (2) like to visit your home, (3) have sharp pains along the course of a nerve?

7. If you were **obsequious**, would it mean that you were:
   (1) seriously ill, (2) slavishly obedient, (3) very cultured?

8. If a person is **indicted**, is he:
   (1) transported from another state for trial, (2) charged with an offense, (3) mentioned for an award for bravery?

9. If the judge was **implacable**, was he:
   (1) relentless, (2) easily pleased, (3) very gruff?

99

Pronunciation

The aim of this lesson is to have the student become acquainted not only with the correct pronunciation of the words in the following list, but also with their definitions.

1. marquee — A canopy projecting over the entrance of a theater or hotel.
2. gondola — Long, narrow boat used in the canals of Venice.
3. alumnae — Girl graduates of a school or college.
4. infamous — Notorious.
5. verbatim — In exactly the same words.
6. vacillate — To waver; to move from one opinion to another.
7. virulent — Extremely poisonous; bitter in enmity.
8. municipal — Pertaining to a city or town.
9. requited — Rewarded; recompensed; given or done in return.
10. rotisserie — A restaurant where patrons may select their meat and see it roasted.

Check Your Pronunciation

1. marquee — mahr key', not mahr qwee'
2. gondola — gon'dola, not gondo'la
3. alumnae — uh lum'nee, not uh lum'nye
4. infamous — in'fuh mus, not infay'mus
5. verbatim — ver bay'tim, not ver bat'im
6. vacillate — vas'il late, not fas'il late
7. virulent — vir'u lent, not vye'ru lent
8. municipal — mu nis'uh pal, not mew'nuh sip'ul
9. requited — re qye'ted, not re quit'ed
10. rotisserie — roe'tees'ree', not roe tis'er ee

Quiz

What word from the preceding list would you use:
1. To describe a robber who has committed many thefts?
2. To describe a person who frequently changes his mind?

3. To convey the idea that the speaker memorized the text?
4. In referring to a good deed that was appreciated or re-warded?
5. To describe a statement that was filled with bitterness?

100

Word Origins

cardinal

The possessive case of the Latin word **cardo,** which means "hinge," is **cardinis.** From its stem is formed the word **cardinal.** A hinge is a very important adjunct to a door; the smoothness with which it opens and closes depends upon its hinge. The adjective **cardinal** is defined as, "chief, important, fundamental." The cardinal points of the compass are the fundamental ones. The noun carries the same implication. The cardinals of the church perform duties of a very significant nature, and often important church questions **hinge** or depend upon their decisions.

posthumous

Many have the mistaken belief that **posthumous** is derived from the Latin **post,** "after," and **humus,** "earth," and that the posthumous writings of an author are those that have been published after he has been buried, that is, placed in the earth. The proper derivation is from the Latin **postumus,** which means "last" and which is the superlative degree of the Latin word **post.**

restaurant

Some years ago, a student who possessed only a slight knowledge of Latin was asked the origin of **restaurant.** He beamed with confidence; he was sure he knew the answer. **Restaurant,** he stated, was composed of the Latin words **res,** "thing," and **taurus,** "bull." Hence, it was a bully thing. No doubt it might mean that to a famished person, but not to a student of etymology. The word comes from the French **restaurer,** or the Latin **restaurare,** meaning "to restore or rebuild." And is not that the purpose of eating, namely, to fortify ourselves or renew our energy with food?

101

Vocabulary Game

Nation Quiz

I

Find a word ending in **nation** for each of the following:

1. A flower.
2. A gift.
3. End.
4. Control by strength or force.
5. Tendency.
6. Explosion.
7. Removal.
8. Inactivity.
9. A pondering.
10. Inoculation.
11. Attraction.
12. Great dismay.
13. Strong disapproval.
14. Great firmness.
15. Occurring by turns.
16. Power of forming mental pictures.
17. The joining of two or more things.
18. A feeling of hate.
19. Resistance to authority.
20. Artful plotting.
21. Patient submission.
22. A place to which a person is going.
23. Murder.
24. Passing the winter.
25. Putting things off until tomorrow.

The first letters of the required words are:

1-c, 2-d, 3-t, 4-d, 5-i, 6-d, 7-e, 8-s, 9-r, 10-v, 11-f, 12-c, 13-c, 14-d, 15-a, 16-i, 17-c, 18-a, 19-i, 20-m, 21-r, 22-d, 23-a, 24-h, 25-p.

II

What word ending in **nation** would you use in each of the following blanks to complete the meaning of the sentence?

1. The laxity of the department in removing snow from the streets aroused the i_____ of the public.

2. There was c_____ among the passengers when the ship began to sink.

3. People of every d_____ contributed to the worthy cause.

4. His being sent to jail was the c_____ of a life of lawlessness.

5. The boy's mother was the i_____ of kindness.

6. His belief that he heard burglars in the house was only a h_____.

102

Clinching Test No. 11

I. *SHOULD* AND *WOULD*

Explain the meaning of the boldface word in each sentence, and then answer the question that is asked. Give the reason for each answer.

1. Should we encourage the use of **archaic** words?

2. Should a leader **vacillate**?

3. Should you do anything that would **imperil** your health?

4. Should a professor try to **infuse** confidence into the minds of his students?

5. Should one use **virulent** language?

6. Should an employer **berate** a faithful worker?

7. Would you call the murder of a child an **infamous** deed?

8. Would you find it difficult to lead an **ascetic** life?

9. Would you have a **nostalgic** feeling if you were away from home for a lengthy period?

10. Would you care to be looked upon as an **obsequious** person?

II. Matching Exercise

For each definition in Column 1, find in Column 2 the word that matches it, and place its number in the blank.

Column 1	Column 2
1. _____ Filthy.	1. repose (*n.*)
2. _____ Showy.	2. imperil
3. _____ To destroy.	3. fusion
4. _____ To endanger.	4. sordid
5. _____ Ease.	5. demolish
6. _____ A union.	6. pretentious

103

Vocabulary Drill

VERBS

Although the majority of the words in the following list may be in the student's recognition or reading vocabulary, nevertheless it would be well for him to give them careful study. The aim of each lesson is to enable the student to include the words being studied in his writing and speaking vocabularies.

deform	To disfigure; to spoil the form of.
efface	To rub out; to destroy; to do away with.
harass	To trouble by repeated attacks; to disturb persistently.
estrange	To make unfriendly; to separate.
delude	To mislead; to trick; to deceive.
assuage	To ease or lessen.
justify	To give a good reason for; to clear of blame.
coalesce	To unite; to grow together.
transcend	To go beyond; to be far superior to.
minimize	To reduce to the least possible degree.
capitalize	To use to one's own advantage.
jeopardize	To endanger; to risk; to expose to loss or injury.

Recasting Exercise

Rewrite the following sentences, incorporating a word from the preceding list that will retain the original meaning of each sentence. The past tense of a verb may be used.

1. We tried hard to help her in her grief.
2. It is hoped the accident will not cripple her.
3. There is a rumor that the three organizations are going to come together as one.
4. If you go out this stormy day, it will not be good for your health.
5. Your fame goes far beyond that of all others in your field.
6. The audience pestered the speaker with many questions.
7. He should make much money through his friendship with the leading politicians.
8. The students were asked to do away with any chalk-writing they saw on buildings or fences.
9. A quarrel over money matters caused the break between the two brothers.
10. Do not let him put you off the track with his glib tongue.
11. He did the right thing in making a complaint.
12. The motorist tried to make as little as possible of the accident in which he was involved.

DEMOLISH

104

Review

Completion Exercise

infuse	justify	demolish
abolish	estrange	admonish

Fill each blank with the noun form of one of the above words to complete the meaning of the sentence. These words have appeared in previous lessons.

1. There was no ————— for his getting so angry at my remark.
2. Money caused the ————— of the two brothers.
3. The incorrigible youngster never heeded the ————— of his parents.
4. The ————— of the old building will start tomorrow.
5. There was a(n) ————— of jealousy in his statement.

Quiz

State your answer for each of these questions.

1. When does a parent **berate** a son or daughter?
2. What syllable in **infamous** receives the accent?
3. What is meant by the **posthumous** work of the author?
4. When is a person **indicted**?
5. What is the **antithesis** of cold?
6. When is a statement given **verbatim**?
7. What is a **diffuse** explanation?
8. When are thoughts **effaced** from one's mind?

105

Achievement-Test Words

I. Matching Exercise

For each word in Column 1, find in Column 2 the definition that matches it, and place its number in the blank preceding the word. (See next page.)

Column 1	Column 2
1. _____ cult	1. Headdress.
2. _____ acme	2. Anticlimax.
3. _____ anent	3. Concerning.
4. _____ regime	4. Short-lived.
5. _____ bathos	5. Nourishment.
6. _____ banal	6. To beautify.
7. _____ juncture	7. Commonplace.
8. _____ coiffure	8. Point of time.
9. _____ globular	9. Globe-shaped.
10. _____ aliment	10. Highest point.
11. _____ embellish	11. System of government.
12. _____ ephemeral	12. System of religious worship.

II. Exercise

1. How does **juncture** differ from **junction?**
2. Is **bathos** a synonym for **pathos?** Explain.
3. Does the last syllable of **coiffure** rhyme with **cure** or **cur?**
4. Show that **perennial** is an antonym for **ephemeral.**
5. Give three pronunciations for **banal.**
6. Explain the meaning of the following sentences:
   a. What he said was **anent** word study.
   b. His writings were **embellished** with many figurative expressions.
   c. He seems to have reached the **acme** of perfection in golf.
   d. He is a member of a **cult** that disapproves of Sunday baseball.

106

Adjectives Pay Dividends

Inasmuch as a speaker or writer is often judged by his use of appropriate adjectives, it will be prudent for every student to endeavor to increase his supply of forceful and worthwhile adjectives.

Study the definitions of the words in the following list in order to be able to do justice to the exercises that follow it.

grave   Serious; solemn; not gay.
fluent   Flowing smoothly; able to write or speak readily.
vivid   Brilliant; distinctly felt; lively.
acute   Sharp; mentally keen; critical.

stable   Firmly established; not easily moved; fixed.
dubious   Doubtful; of uncertain event or issue.
vigilant   Watchful; alert.
defiant   Bold; insolent; openly resisting.

ostensible Apparent; pretended; avowed.
indolent   Lazy; disliking work or exertion.
relentless Unyielding; stern; mercilessly harsh.
superfluous Needless; more than is required.

I. Drill

Fill each blank with the word that will make the sentence correct. The answers should be associated with the words in the above list.

1. The noun form of **grave** is _____.
2. **Stabilize** is the _____ form of **stable**.
3. The prefix **super** in **superfluous** means _____.
4. An antonym for **merciful** is _____.
5. There was an _____ shortage of rubber during World War II.
6. **Revivify** and **vivify** are related in meaning to _____.
7. The noun form of **fluent** is _____.
8. **Real** is an antonym for _____.

II. Completion Quiz

Which of the words in the preceding list would you use to describe:

1. A student who dislikes to study? _____
2. A ruler who is very severe? _____
3. A government that is very strong? _____
4. Colors that are extremely bright? _____
5. A severe pain in the side? _____
6. A people that refuses to obey their leader? _____

[135]

7. A speaker who expresses his thoughts easily? _____
8. A situation that seems to indicate trouble? _____
9. A dog that closely guards a house? _____
10. A statement that has already been made? _____
11. An election the results of which are very close and uncertain? _____
12. A professed but not a real reason? _____

Exercise

1. Construct original sentences with the following phrases:

acute mind	stable prices
acute situation	stable furniture
acute sense of humor	stable foundation
grave colors	vivid red
grave problem	vivid description
grave responsibility	vivid recollection

2. Use in original sentences: **relent**; **stability**.
3. Give three words which contain the prefix **super**.

VIGILANT

[136]

107

Vocabulary Review Exercise

Explain the meaning of each of the following sentences.

1. The rebels worked **relentlessly** to overthrow the government.

2. He was punished for acting so **defiantly**.

3. The lives of the firemen were in **jeopardy** during the big fire.

4. **Profuse** praise was showered on the football hero.

5. The student **vividly** described the first act of the play.

6. The people were **ostensibly** affected by the death of their governor.

What Is Your Answer?

1. When is a woman **pretentiously** dressed?
2. How can a home be **embellished**?
3. What is an **acute** mind?
4. What is the noun form of **grave**?
5. What is the price of **indolence** at school or college?
6. What is a **superfluous** statement? Can you give an example of one?
7. Why should every city have a **vigilant** police department?

108

Clinching Test No. 12

I. Exercise

1. Prove that **sediment, supersede,** and **sedentary** stem from the same root.
2. Write three words which contain the prefix **subter** or **sub.**
3. Give the two recorded pronunciations for **sinecure.**
4. Use the verb-form of **predominant** in a sentence.

[137]

II. Pronunciation

Fill each blank with the appropriate word:

1. Clandestine is accented on the _____ syllable.

2. Decade is accented on the _____ syllable, and its last syllable rhymes with _____.

3. The _____ syllable of **virago** receives the accent. This syllable should rhyme with _____.

4. The first syllable of **succinct** is pronounced _____.

5. The last syllable of **cortege** is pronounced as though it were spelled _____ and not **tidge**.

III. Completion Exercise

deform	harass	ostensibly
stable (*adj.*)	efface	capitalize
vivid	embellish	superfluous

Select a word from the above list to complete the meaning of each of the following sentences:

1. He will never be able to _____ that tragic scene from his memory.

2. A statement that is not necessary is called _____.

3. The collegian is trying to _____ on his athletic ability.

4. Do not _____ the professor with so many questions.

5. The noun form of **deform** is _____.

6. There is a _____ currency in that country.

7. His family, despite their hardships, is _____ happy.

8. He tried to _____ his talk with a few personal experiences.

9. The young girl gave a _____ account of her trip.

IV. Multiple-Choice Exercise

Select the word or expression which best defines the boldface word:

1. A **sedentary** position:
(a) easy, (b) important, (c) requiring much sitting.

2. Result of the **orgy**:
(a) musicale, (b) carousal, (c) injury.

3. Too **repetitious** to be interesting:
(a) long, (b) forceful, (c) tiresomely repeating.

4. A **dispassionate** view of the case:
   (a) impartial, (b) hot-tempered, (c) without zeal.
5. His sickness was a **subterfuge**:
   (a) caused a postponement, (b) not serious, (c) trick to escape something unpleasant.
6. **Tyrannized** over his subjects:
   (a) ruled severely, (b) made them tyrants, (c) appeased.
7. Sought a tax **exemption**:
   (a) reduction, (b) release, (c) increase.
8. Desired a **sinecure**:
   (a) easy job, (b) remedy, (c) promotion.
9. A **predominant** position:
   (a) slavish, (b) dictatorial, (c) superior.
10. A **surreptitious** act:
    (a) done secretly, (b) unpopular, (c) repeated.
11. It **revolutionized** travel:
    (a) made it dangerous, (b) impeded, (c) changed completely.
12. Changed his **perspective**:
    (a) over-all view, (b) mind, (c) eyeglasses.

109

Words Taken from Achievement Tests

Recasting Exercise

contrite	sorrowful	**discursive**	rambling
senile	of old age	**delectable**	enjoyable
dearth	scarcity	**audacious**	daring
canard	false rumor	**mendicant**	beggar
fallible	liable to err	**charlatan**	a quack
decorum	proper conduct	**philatelist**	stamp collector

Rewrite the following sentences, using the words from the above list to retain the original meaning of each sentence. The boldface words may help you to select the proper terms.

1. There is a **scarcity** of doctors in that country.

2. We partook of a very **enjoyable** meal.

3. The students were urged **to act politely and properly** during their trip.

4. Many people were deluded by the philosophy of the **pretended statesman.**

5. We are all **susceptible to making mistakes.**

6. There were many **people soliciting funds for themselves** in the big city.

7. The rumor that war would soon be declared was **absolutely false.**

8. The speaker seemed to **deviate altogether too much from his topic.**

9. She made a **rather sorrowful** confession of her part in the conspiracy.

10. The burglar made a **bold** attempt to rob the bank in the daytime.

11. His irrational statements might be attributed to his **old age.**

12. My brother likes **to collect stamps.**

110

Verbs Ending in "ate"

The verbs in this lesson have such a pleasant sound and are of such a practical nature that the student should endeavor to integrate them into his working vocabulary as quickly as possible. A careful study of the definitions below will make this achievement a reality.

alienate	To turn against; to divert, as affection or confidence.
obliterate	To blot out; to remove all trace of.
fluctuate	To waver; to rise and fall; to change continually.
conciliate	To win over; to bring into harmony; to please.
simulate	To have the appearance of; to pretend.
remunerate	To reward; to pay for services.

assimilate	To absorb; to digest.
disintegrate	To break up; to separate into small parts.
calumniate	To accuse falsely; to slander.
disseminate	To scatter widely; to spread abroad.
necessitate	To make necessary; to force; to demand.
incapacitate	To render unfit; to disable; to disqualify.

Quiz

What word from the preceding list would you use to convey the idea or thought:

1. That you tried to drive away from your mind all thoughts of the accident?

2. That you will be paid for the services or work you perform?

3. That your friend's good name was blackened?

4. That your hopes rise and fall periodically?

5. That your age will not permit you to play football?

6. That you should spread abroad the information you have of your friends' good deeds?

111

Pronunciation

Here is another list of words which, with one or two exceptions, are frequently seen and heard. The phoneticized forms should make the assignment easy and understandable for the student. Learn the definitions as well as the pronunciations.

1.	**chasm**	Deep opening in the earth; wide difference of feelings.
2.	**ghoul**	A grave robber; one who enjoys what is horrible.
3.	**adobe**	Sun-dried brick; clay for such brick.
4.	**bayou**	A marshy inlet or outlet of a lake, river, or gulf.
5.	**covert**	Secret; disguised; hidden.

[141]

6. galaxy	A brilliant group.
7. mayoralty	Position of mayor; his term of office.
8. blackguard	A scoundrel.
9. disheveled	Disordered, untidy.
10. inflammable	Easily set on fire; easily excited.

Study

chasm	kaz′um, not chaz′um
ghoul	gool, not gowhl
adobe	adoe′be, not ad′obe
bayou	bye′oo, not bay′oo
covert	kuv′ert, not koe′vert
galaxy	gal′ux se, not galax′si
mayoralty	may′er ul ty, not may′er al′i ty
blackguard	blag′ard, not black′guard
disheveled	dishev′uld, not dis hev′eld
inflammable	in flam′uh b′l, not in flame′uh b′l

112

Vocabulary Game

TUDE WORDS

Our language is replete with words ending in **tude** which the student should endeavor to cultivate for use in his active vocabulary. The answer to each of the following riddles should end in **tude**. The first letter of the required word is given.

1. We use it in talking about mountains and airplanes. **A**
2. What Henry Thoreau, who lived an isolated life, liked and enjoyed. **S**
3. It is often employed in reference to the size of our national debt. **M**
4. Mothers felt this when their sons were at war. **S**
5. We all experience a touch of it in the springtime. **L**
6. It was possessed by our pioneers. **F**
7. An expression which is threadbare from overuse. **P**
8. It is the measure of worldly goods you would like to possess. **P**

9. It should characterize your appearance at school and readiness in acting. **P**

10. It is what every girl would like to possess. **P**

11. It is what one seeks in spending his vacation in the country. **Q**

12. It was the state in which many were found after ancient wars. **S**

13. It is the name of a test to ascertain what line of activity a student shows a fitness for. **A**

14. A word that may be applied to the ups and downs of life. **V**

15. A state in which a 1917 Ford would likely be found. **D**

16. You have it when you are absolutely positive or certain about something. **C**

17. It is what usually appears when the President speaks out-of-doors. **M**

18. It is often used as, "Give him an _____ of rope and he will hang himself." **A**

113

Clinching Test No. 13

I. Matching Exercise

For each word in Column 1, find in Column 2 the definition that matches it, and place its number in the blank.

Column 1	*Column 2*
1. _____ contrite	1. Hidden.
2. _____ covert	2. Daring.
3. _____ mendicant	3. Beggar.
4. _____ calumniate	4. Temperate.
5. _____ obliterate	5. To wipe out.
6. _____ disintegrate	6. Sorrowful.
7. _____ abstemious	7. To slander.
8. _____ disseminate	8. To break up.
9. _____ audacious	9. To spread widely.

II. Pronunciation Exercise

Fill each blank with a word or letter which will make the sentence correct:
1. The **ch** in **chasm** is sounded like the letter _____.
2. The second syllable in **disheveled** is _____.
3. The third letter in **remunerate** is _____, not **n**.
4. **Adobe** is accented on the _____ syllable.
5. The second syllable in **inflammable** rhymes with _____ ___ and not with **blame**.

III. Multiple-Choice Exercise

Select the word or expression that best defines the boldface word:

1. A **delectable** meal. (1) enjoyable, (2) costly, (3) heavy.

2. A **discursive** writer. (1) controversial, (2) scholarly, (3) rambling.

3. An **inflammable** substance. (1) light, (2) not ignitable, (3) easily set on fire.

4. Enthusiasm that was **simulated**. (1) aroused, (2) pretended, (3) lacking.

5. **Decorum** was missing. (1) good conduct, (2) decorations, (3) flattery.

6. A **dearth** of news. (1) abundance, (2) dislike, (3) scarcity.

7. **Simulated** knowledge. (1) pretended, (2) acquired, (3) unnecessary.

114

Vocabulary Exercise

ADJECTIVES

Every student who desires to improve his vocabulary should endeavor to accumulate a reasonably large supply of adjectives. Study the definitions of the following adjectives.

[144]

habitual	Done by habit; customary.
dormant	Inactive; quiet as if asleep.
inherent	Belonging by nature or habit.
salutary	Beneficial; wholesome.
mangled	Torn; mutilated.
feasible	Capable of being done.
divergent	Different; characterized by disagreement.
expeditious	Quick; speedy.
perennial	Lasting; recurring annually.
nefarious	Very wicked; villainous.
incongruous	Inconsistent; out of place.
co-operative	Willing to work together with others.

Completion Exercise

Fill each blank with a word from the preceding list to complete the meaning of the sentence:

1. The professor's talk had a _____ effect upon the class.
2. The success of the project demanded _____ action.
3. Their _____ opinions kept the two factions apart.
4. She wears such _____ colors as to evoke laughter from her friends.
5. The antagonism between the two families has been _____ for the past five years.
6. The desire to do good seemed to be _____ in him even when he was a child.
7. The public received only a _____ report of the meeting.
8. Her _____ smile won her many friends.

115

Words Frequently Confused

By learning the definitions of the words in this lesson you will be able to discern the differences in the meanings of the words in each pair and at the same time add them to your active vocabulary.

beneficent   Doing good; performing acts of kindness.
beneficial   Profitable; helpful; advantageous.

His many **beneficent** acts for the poor were never publicized.
You will find a large vocabulary most **beneficial** when you are out in the world of activity.
The climate proved **beneficial** to the sick boy.

venal   Corrupt; willing to sell one's service; open to bribes.
venial   Pardonable; not very wrong; slight.

Politicians should not resort to **venal** practices.
The error was of only a **venial** nature.

etymology   The study of words and their derivations.
entomology   The study of insects.

What is the **etymology** of *autograph?*
He has taken two courses in **entomology.**

intelligible   Capable of being understood.

intelligent   Able to learn and understand; showing understanding.

That young man, although only three months in this country, could use **intelligible** English.
The writer's style is so profound, I am sure that what he says is **unintelligible** to many of his readers.
The child gave an **intelligent** answer.

remedial   Affording a remedy; helpful.
remediable   Capable of being cured or corrected.

Every student should take **remedial** measures to improve his vocabulary.
The crippled youngster is receiving **remedial** treatment.
Your weakness in reading is **remediable** and could be overcome with a little extra effort.
The mistake was **remediable.**

(The second syllable in each word is **me** and should rhyme with **bee**.)

116

Synonyms

I

add	suppose	dislike	seeking
true	caught	associates (*n.*)	uphold
clever	arrange	attacked	stillness

In the above list the student will find an answer to each of the following questions. The answer will be in the nature of a synonym for the boldface word.

1. When is a story **authentic?**
2. What is an **astute** answer?
3. When does a student have an **aversion** to study?
4. What is meant by the **quietude** of the country?
5. What would you do if you were asked to **classify** the names of people according to their occupations?
6. When is a person **soliciting** contributions?
7. When you **assume** that a thing is right, what do you do?
8. When is a statement **assailed?**
9. When does the Senate **sanction** an appointment?
10. When are people considered **colleagues?**
11. When is a thief **apprehended?**
12. When does one **append** a note to a letter?

II

Tell whether each word at the right is a synonym or an antonym of the word in the left column:

1. **insidious**   deceitful, guileless, tricky
2. **judicious**   indiscreet, imprudent, sagacious
3. **emanate**   issue, suppress, radiate
4. **confirm**   verify, invalidate, substantiate
5. **tenable**   valid, defensible, worthless

Words Taken from Achievement Tests

Multiple-Choice Exercise

Select the word or expression that most nearly defines the boldface word. For the correct answers, be sure to consult the dictionary.

1. An **insipid** discourse:
   (a) dull, (b) very short, (c) very sad.
2. A **perjured** statement:
   (a) premeditated, (b) colorless, (c) false under oath.
3. He was **exonerated**:
   (a) blamed for, (b) failed, (c) proved innocent.
4. Worked **scrupulously**:
   (a) very carefully, (b) indifferently, (c) slowly.
5. Possessed a **magnanimous** spirit:
   (a) selfish, (b) rebellious, (c) noble.
6. Slang was **deprecated**:
   (a) used extensively, (b) disapproved of, (c) overlooked.
7. **Expedited** by them:
   (a) accrued, (b) hastened, (c) postponed.
8. Presented in a **jocose** way:
   (a) uninteresting, (b) humorous, (c) fleeting.
9. Exhibited **churlish** characteristics:
   (a) immature, (b) feminine, (c) surly.
10. A **vituperative** editorial:
    (a) abusive, (b) full of life, (c) profound.
11. Punctuated with **derisive** remarks:
    (a) cutting, (b) ridiculing, (c) uplifting.
12. A **deleterious** effect:
    (a) harmful, (b) unexpected, (c) unjustified.

Pronunciation Helps

1. In **churlish**, the **ch** is pronounced like the **ch** in **church** and not as in **character**.
2. The second syllable in **derisive, ri,** should rhyme with **my** and not with **miss**.

3. In **magnanimous,** the second syllable, which is accented, is **nan.**

4. **Jocose** is accented on the last syllable.

5. The **i** in **vi,** the first syllable in **vituperative,** may be long or short.

118

Word Origins

focus

The Latin for "fireplace" is **focus.** Years ago when families did not sardine themselves in apartment houses and when furnace heat was unknown, each home had a large living room in which was a fireplace or **focus.** In this room before the fire the members would assemble in the evening. Hence, we derive the meaning of "central point" or "center of attraction or activity" from the word **focus.**

nicotine

This word takes its name from a Frenchman named Jean Nicot, who introduced tobacco into France in 1560.

cathedral

The word for "seat" in Greek is **cathedra,** which refers to the episcopal, or **bishop's, chair.** Hence, **cathedral** means the principal church in the diocese or district which contains the bishop's seat or throne.

umpire

Par, in Latin as well as in the language of the golfer, means "equal." **Nonpar** would then be defined as "not equal." This definition is ambiguous, as it may convey the idea of inferiority or superiority, depending upon the speaker's point of view. However, **non par** came to be used in the sense of "superior." Hence, in a game **non par** denoted a person "above" the others, whose decisions were to be accepted. It is very likely that rapid pronunciation and ignorance of its origin are responsible for the present distorted form, **umpire.**

119

Vocabulary Game

MAL WORDS

Rewrite each of the following sentences, incorporating in it a word beginning with **mal** that will retain the original meaning of the sentence. The words to be selected are found following the sentences. The past tense of a verb and the plural of a noun may be used if necessary.

1. The child was badly formed as a result of the accident.
2. He never seemed satisfied at the way things were done
3. The salaries in that organization are poorly arranged.
4. He tried to injure his friend's reputation.
5. That boy always feigns sickness in order to escape work.
6. Lincoln asked that we show no ill will to the conquered.
7. For his many evil deeds he was committed to jail.
8. We all agreed that the remark came at the wrong time.
9. The governor was impeached for official misconduct.
10. He always seemed to wish that evil would happen to us.
11. There was no need of heaping curses on those who opposed him.
12. We were all affected with seasickness during the voyage.
13. The plantation owner was very cruel to those who worked for him.
14. The child is suffering from improper nourishment.
15. The fruit in the cupboard has a very bad smell.

The answers may be selected from the following words:

malice	malapropos	malingerer	malefaction
malign	malcontent	mal-de-mer	malediction
maltreat	maladjusted	malodorous	malnutrition
malformed	malfeasance	malevolent	

Clinching Test No. 14

Completion Exercise I

dormant   salutary   propensity
suspend   impending   malefactor
divergent   perennial   intelligible

Fill each blank with a word from the preceding list to complete the meaning of the sentence:

1. English that cannot be understood cannot be called _____.

2. To delay operation on a project is to _____ work on it.

3. If a boy delights in manual work, he may be said to have a _____ for it.

4. One who commits an evil deed may be called a _____.

5. Theories that do not agree may be referred to as _____ ones.

6. Energy or ability that has been inactive for a time and which can be aroused may be called _____.

7. Complaints which arise yearly or periodically may be labelled _____ complaints.

8. The talk had a _____ effect upon the student body.

9. Dark clouds usually symbolize an _____ storm.

II. Synonym Exercise

untenable   insipid   etymology
assailed   perjured   vituperative

Substitute a synonym from the above list for each boldface word or group of words in the following sentences:

1. That speech will be **attacked** by the people.
2. What is the **derivation** of that word?
3. He **told a lie while under oath** on the witness stand.
4. The story he narrated was of a **dull** nature.
5. The fort was **not capable of being defended.**
6. It was an **abusive** editorial.

121

Vocabulary

I. Matching Exercise

In Column 2 are definitions of the words in Column 1. Number each definition the same as the word it defines. Be sure to check your answers with a dictionary. This will not require much time, inasmuch as the list of words is alphabetized.

I

Column 1	*Column 2*
1. abate	1. _____ Disposed to attack.
2. adjacent	2. _____ To cheat.
3. affect	3. _____ To empty.
4. aggressive	4. _____ Qualified to be chosen.
5. appraise	5. _____ To reduce in intensity.
6. brevity	6. _____ To break up.
7. defraud	7. _____ To judge as to quality.
8. deplete	8. _____ Situated near or next.
9. disrupt	9. _____ Conciseness in speech or writing.
10. eligible	10. _____ To produce a change or effect upon.

II

11. facility	11. _____ Vast.
12. prodigious	12. _____ To rise.
13. reconcile	13. _____ To prove to be correct.
14. renounce	14. _____ Easily influenced by emotions.
15. retard	15. _____ To overcome.
16. surge (*v.*)	16. _____ Power to do something easily.
17. surmount	17. _____ To give up entirely.
18. susceptible	18. _____ To hold power by force.
19. usurp	19. _____ To bring into harmony.
20. verify	20. _____ To delay the progress of.

II. Checking Exercise

What word from the preceding list would you use:

1. To express the thought that the pain had lessened?
2. To describe a marvelous memory?
3. To indicate that a poor vocabulary may prove a hindrance to success?
4. To state that your anger was aroused?
5. To mean that a person will accept a bribe?
6. To say that the talk was not too long?
7. To describe a person who is quarrelsome?
8. To convey the idea that you were cheated in the sale?
9. To state that the law pertains to all people?
10. To assert that the leader assumed the duties of office by force?
11. To state that you would be able to overcome any difficulties that might appear?
12. To say that you could prove that the report was correct?

122

Words Frequently Confused

I. Matching Exercise

For each definition in Column 1, find in Column 2 the word that matches it, and place its number in the blank preceding the definition. (See next page.)

Column 1	Column 2
1. _____ A group of persons.	1. **marital**
2. _____ Greediness.	2. **martial**
3. _____ Refers to size; natural height.	3. **augur**
4. _____ Pertaining to a husband or marriage.	4. **auger**
5. _____ A tool for boring holes.	5. **statute**
6. _____ One endowed with great ability or inventiveness.	6. **stature**
7. _____ A slight, sharp sound.	7. **click**
8. _____ Truthfulness.	8. **clique**
9. _____ To foretell; to prophesy.	9. **genus**
10. _____ Pertaining to war.	10. **genius**
11. _____ A group, kind, or classification.	11. **veracity**
12. _____ A law established by the legislative branch.	12. **voracity**

II. Exercise

Explain the following:

1. The lion, tiger, and lynx belong to the same **genus**.
2. Mary is a **voracious** reader.
3. **Martial** music was played.
4. It was a **veracious** report.
5. Such careful planning **augurs** success.

123

Words Taken from Achievement Tests

MULTIPLE USES OF WORDS

malign To speak ill of.
inhibit To forbid; to hinder.
prodigal Wasteful; luxuriant.

lacerate To mangle; to distress.
dominate To rule by strength or power.

[154]

concur To agree; to co-operate; to occur at the same time.

emergence A rising from.
ostentatious Showy; done for display.

Fill each blank with a word taken from the preceding list or with some other part of speech of a word from this list. When the latter is required, the first letter of the desired word will be given. Some of the words above will be used more than once.

1. You will _____ with me that the plan is workable.
2. The great harvest shows how _____ Nature is.
3. His parents placed too many i_____ on him.
4. Mr. Brown is one of the d_____ leaders in our country.
5. One can detect an _____ of good times.
6. We should never _____ either our friends or our foes.
7. The cat _____ the baby's face.
8. If the members all _____, the drive will be a success.
9. The big boys often try to _____ the little children.
10. She should not wear such _____ clothes.
11. The teacher gave me a l_____ look when I spilled the ink.
12. We must consider the e_____ generation when we plan a school-building program.
13. The average person dislikes o_____.
14. Do not _____ your children from expressing themselves.
15. The class was treated to a _____ meal.
16. The dictator's aim was world d_____.
17. Keeping company with that gang had a m_____ influence on John.
18. The two lectures were delivered c_____.
19. We cannot attend both courses because they _____.
20. A good speaker never uses words o_____.

124

Synonyms

Fill each blank with a synonym for the boldface word at the top of each group. The first letter of the required synonym is given. This assignment may not prove so easy as it appears.

fat

1. Mary has become very s_____.
2. His sister is small and p_____.
3. You are becoming too c_____.
4. Henry VIII was a p_____ individual.

love (v.)

5. We did not l_____ the show.
6. The girls i_____ that young actor.
7. Did anyone a_____ your hat?
8. The children seem to a_____ their parents.

active

9. One should be p_____ with his appointments.
10. Football players must be a_____ for fumbles by their opponents.
11. A v_____ eye must be kept upon that country.
12. Mr. Jones has three very l_____ children.

near

13. New Jersey b_____ the State of New York.
14. Mary and Josephine are very c_____ friends.
15. Their property a_____ ours.
16. A cemetery was a_____ to the church.

arrange

17. The potatoes were a_____ according to size.
18. The applicants will be l_____ according to age and experience.
19. It will be necessary to a_____ the salaries of our teachers.
20. The children were g_____ according to grade.

Words Frequently Confused

To become adept in the use of words, it is necessary to have a firm grasp and understanding of the definitions of words that bear a close resemblance to one another in pronunciation or in spelling. Study carefully the definitions of the word-pairs in this lesson.

seasonal   Related to or influenced by certain periods of the year.

seasonable   Occurring or coming in good or proper time; opportune.

Hot weather in October in the New England States is not **seasonable**. (It is not the month for high temperatures.)

The advice to the graduating class was **seasonable**. (It was the opportune time, inasmuch as the graduates were about to take their place in various fields of activity.)

Baseball is a **seasonal** sport. (It is played only in the summer months.)

formerly   In time past; heretofore.

formally   In a formal manner; according to established custom.

This work was **formerly** done by the principal of the school.
All dressed **formally** for the dance.

stationary   Fixed; not moving.

stationery   Writing material.

The furniture in the classroom is **stationary.**
You will find the **stationery** on my desk.

(Stationery includes *pens, pencils,* and *paper.* Note that the letter **e** appears in each of these three words. Hence, if reference is made to writing material, be sure to spell the word with an **e.**)

egoism   Excessive thought or love of self; regarding oneself as the center of every interest.

egotism   The practice of speaking or writing too much about oneself; self-praise.

(The difference between these words is that **egoism** is ascribed to a person who thinks much of himself; **egotism**, to one who not only thinks much of self, but also gives expression, either in speaking or writing, to this high esteem of self. The first syllable may be **e** or **eg** for both words.)

126

Pronunciation

ADDED FORMS

The following words, prior to the publication of *Webster's New Collegiate Dictionary* in 1949, were restricted to one correct pronunciation. Since that date, another form of pronunciation has been given to each word.

1. quay	3. entirety	5. gardenia
2. traverse	4. cerebral	6. precedence

1. Few people could understand why **quay** had to be pronounced **key**. All are happy now to know that it may also be pronounced to rhyme with **bay**.

2. No longer is one asked to accent the first syllable of **traverse**. It is equally correct to place the accent on the last syllable.

3. **Entire** is a word of two syllables. Consequently, the dictionary-makers for years gave only three syllables to **entirety**. One may now pronounce it as a word of four syllables.

4. That **cerebral** may henceforth be pronounced both **cer'ebral** and **ceree'bral** will be pleasant news to the many persons who always gave this word the latter pronunciation, which did not receive the approval of the dictionary-compilers until 1949.

5. The name of the fragrant flower **gardenia** may be pronounced as a word of four syllables or three syllables. The form **gar deen'ya** is now accepted.

6. Although **precedence** was very frequently pronounced **pres'e dense**, that form was not recorded until recently.

Either the second syllable or the first may now receive the accent.

Exercise

Explain the meaning of each of the following sentences.

1. The **quay** was badly damaged by the hurricane.
2. We **traversed** that section of the city almost daily.
3. The lesson must be learned in its **entirety**.
4. The victim of the fight suffered a **cerebral** hemorrhage.
5. She wore a corsage of **gardenias**.
6. At the banquet table **precedence** was given to the wives of the officers.

Worth Knowing

hospitable   restaurant   coupon

The pronunciations **hospit′able, res′toe rahnt,** and **koo′pon,** although found in the *Webster's New Collegiate Dictionary,* are labelled British forms.

127

Root Words

If the student were to study the various English words that are derived from the two-syllable Latin word **duco,** he would be amazed at their number. A few of the derivatives are presented in this exercise.

duco (*pres. tense*), **ductus** (*past part.*), to lead; to bring forth. (Stem: **duc** or **duct**)

Matching Exercise

For each definition in Column 1, find in Column 2 the word that matches it, and place its number in the blank preceding the definition. (See next page.)

Column 1	Column 2
1. _____ To bring down.	1. educe
2. _____ To take away.	2. induce
3. _____ Incentive.	3. reduce
4. _____ To prevail upon.	4. seduce
5. _____ To draw out.	5. deduct
6. _____ An inference; subtraction.	6. conduct (*v.*)
	7. educate
7. _____ To draw out; to lead by.	8. aqueduct
8. _____ To lead or guide.	9. introduce
9. _____ Bringing forth; fertile.	10. deduction
10. _____ To lead into error or crime.	11. productive
	12. inducement
11. _____ To bring in; to make known.	
12. _____ An artificial channel for bringing water from a distance.	

erro (*pres. tense*), **erratus** (*past part.*), to wander. (Stem: **err** or **errat**)

When one makes a mistake, he wanders away from the right course.

Exercise

Study the uses of the boldface words in the following exercise in order to be able to place them in original sentences:

1. When a baseball outfielder misses a fly ball, he is charged with an **error**.

2. When a person is eccentric or follows no certain course, he is called **erratic**.

3. When one makes a mistake, he **errs**.

4. When a person's reasoning is wrong, it is labeled **erroneous**.

5. When a mistake is made in printing or writing, it is called an **erratum**.

6. When there is a wandering from the standard or regular course, it is referred to as an **aberration**.

7. When beliefs deviate from the truth they are of an **errant** nature.

[160]

8. When you read of the chivalrous, adventurous men of the early centuries, the author very likely called them knights-errant.

128

Word Origins

parasite

The Greek word **parasitos** was interpreted as "one eating beside another." Today this word implies "eating on or at the expense of another." Originally, **parasites** were people who because of their humor or ready conversation were invited to be guests at the tables of the rich.

ballot

Long before present-day voting machines came into use, secret voting was done by dropping small balls into a box. This custom still exists in some of our fraternal organizations when there is balloting upon candidates for membership. You have often heard the expression, "They blackballed Mr. X at the last meeting," which means that someone was denied membership because of the number of black balls placed in the box that contained his name. **Ballot** is from the Italian **balla,** which means "ball" and referred to the ball which signified a vote.

love

This is not the **love** that exists between boy and girl, but rather it is a term used in tennis. Have you not often wondered why the scoring in tennis runs **40-love**, or **love-40** and so on? In tennis, **love** means "nothing." Thus, **40-love** means 40 to nothing; **love-30,** nothing to 30. The first number of the score refers to the person who serves. The question is, how did **love** descend to the depths of zero or nothingness? Here is the story. The French word for egg, whose shape resembles a zero, is **l'oeuf.** This term gradually changed in sound to **love.**

precocious

You have heard stern and very strict leaders referred to as "hard-boiled" persons. One such person can be found in every city. But does your city contain "an early-cooked child?" The term applied to such a prodigy is **precocious**. This word stems from the Latin **pre**, "before," and **coquere**, to cook. Hence, a **precocious** child is one of early maturity. The dictionary definition is "exceptionally early in mental development."

129

Clinching Test No. 15

I. Why?

Explain the meaning of the boldface word in each sentence, and then answer the question that is asked.

1. Why should we never **malign** people?

2. Why should you not try to **dominate** the members of your club?

3. Why are **corpulent** students poor material for a football team?

4. Why is skating considered a **seasonal** sport?

5. Why should one refrain from wearing **ostentatious** clothes?

6. Why should you endeavor never to be **egotistic**?

II. Completion Exercise

concur	retard	lacerate
deplete	surmount	aggressive
disrupt	prodigious	susceptible

Fill each blank with a word from the above list to complete the meaning of the sentence:

1. Such a vast undertaking would _____ our treasury.

2. All soon realized that our leader was not _____ to graft.

3. Our professor of English has a _____ memory.

4. Our country needs more _____ leaders in the various fields of government.

5. How did the child _____ his hand?

6. He had to _____ many difficulties.

7. She realized that a poor vocabulary would _____ her progress.

8. The agitator did his utmost to _____ the meeting.

9. We must all _____ in order to make the project a success.

130

Vocabulary

mystify	To puzzle; to bewilder.
plausible	Apparently reasonable or true.
detriment	Handicap; harm; damage.
ponderous	Weighty; dull.
pernicious	Highly injurious; very harmful.
invigorate	To give strength to.
phlegmatic	Sluggish; not easily moved.
intolerable	Unbearable; insufferable.
lamentable	Pitiable; mournful.
omnivorous	Eating both animal and vegetable rood.
peremptory	Positive; decisive.
invalidate	To make valueless; to destroy the strength of.

Completion Exercise

Fill each blank in the following sentences with a word from the above list that will complete the meaning of the sentence. It would be helpful to the student if he would then place these words in original sentences.

1. Man is an _____ animal.

2. A lawbreaker is a _____ to society.

3. Such conduct will _____ your parents.

[163]

4. The trip to the country seemed to _____ my sister.

5. John's poor marks proved that he was a _____ failure in college.

6. The absence of their signatures will _____ the contract.

7. Such _____ teaching may cause great harm to our country.

8. He discovered that the duties of his department were too _____ for one man to shoulder.

9. She did not possess many friends because of her slow and _____ nature.

10. Many emigrated from that country because of the _____ cruelty of the leaders.

11. All dictators resort to _____ procedures if necessary to achieve their ends.

12. A _____ remedy for our present trouble was submitted by our local senator.

131

Pronunciation

ADDED FORMS

The words in this lesson were given two pronunciations when the 1949 edition of *Webster's New Collegiate Dictionary* was published.

aviation The pronunciation frequently heard, although not heretofore recorded in the dictionary, was **av'iation.** Formerly it was necessary to have the first syllable **a** rhyme with **play.** Now it is also correct to have it rhyme with **have.** The same change applies to **aviator.**

digitalis Rarely did one hear this word, which is the name of a heart stimulant, pronounced so that the third syllable **ta** rhymed with **say.** Still that was the only form recorded in most dictionaries. Although **digitay'lis** is still correct, the present preferred pronunciation is to have the syllable rhyme with **pal,** that is, **digital'is.**

impetigo The third syllable in **impetigo,** the name of a skin disease, may now be pronounced **tie,** as formerly, or **tee.**

khaki Although formerly the first syllable rhymed with **block,** one may now have it rhyme with **tack** and be correct.

forehead In addition to the always correct pronunciation **for'ed,** one may now sound the letter **h: for'head,** and be correct.

culinary No doubt people were more interested in what this word implied, namely, "kitchen or cooking," than in its correct pronunciation. Henceforth one may sound the first syllable like the letter **q** or let it rhyme with **dull: cue'linary** or **cul'inary.**

applicable It will be good news to many students and adults to learn that it is no longer incorrect to accent the second syllable of this word. Both **ap'plicable** and **applic'able** are correct.

132

Pronunciation

Since every word in the following list contains a degree of difficulty, it will be to the student's profit to study the list very carefully. The definitions should also be learned.

1.	**epitome**	Summary.
2.	**quietus**	End.
3.	**vanilla**	A flavoring extract.
4.	**credence**	Belief.
5.	**puerile**	Foolish; childish.
6.	**imbroglio**	Disagreement; a confused situation.
7.	**longevity**	Great length of life.
8.	**pyramidal**	Having the form of a pyramid.

9. **lamentable**   Deplorable; regrettable; mournful.
10. **incongruous**   Inconsistent; not appropriate.

Check Your Pronunciation

1. epitome   uh pit'uh me, not ep'uh tome.
2. quietus   qye ee'tus, not qye'uh tus.
3. vanilla   vuh nil'uh, not vuh nel'uh.
4. credence   kree'dense, not kred'ense.
5. puerile   pew'er il, not pure'il.
6. imbroglio   im broel'yoe, not im broeg'le oh.
◦ 7. longevity   lahn jev'uh ty, not long gev'uh ty.
8. pyramidal   per am'uh dul, not peer'uh mid'ul.
9. lamentable   lam'entable, not lament'able.
10. incongruous   incon'gruous, not incongru'ous.

Completion Exercise

Fill each blank with a word from the preceding list to complete the sentence. Read each sentence aloud.

1. The class was asked to give an _____ of the play.
2. He attributed his _____ to proper and careful living.
3. Fur coats are _____ in the hot weather.
4. His _____ story won our sympathy.
5. We placed no _____ in what he said.
6. The police put a _____ to the fight.
7. No one paid any attention to the _____ remarks of the speaker.
8. The speaker referred to the _____ shape of the building.

133

Vocabulary Game

I. *ACIOUS* WORDS

Name the word that ends in **acious**:
1. Which means quick to fight. **P**
2. Which describes a very talkative person. **L**

3. Which is an antonym for dull or listless. **V**
4. Which conveys the thought of boldness. **A**
5. Which refers to robbery. **R**
6. Which is used to describe lewd and indecent writing. **S**
7. Which may be applied to a very good memory. **T**

II. *ANCE* WORDS

The answer to each question should end in **ance**.

1. Beginning with **R**, it denotes hesitation.
2. Beginning with **I**, it is the opposite of moderation.
3. Beginning with **R**, it expresses extreme dislike.
4. Beginning with **L**, it refers to an abundant growth.
5. Beginning with **C**, it denotes pretended ignorance or secret encouragement of wrongdoing.
6. Beginning with **A**, it means a state of suspended action.
7. Beginning with **T**, it is what we should practice toward other people whose opinions differ from ours.

III. *LENT* WORDS

What word ending in **lent** would you substitute for the bold-face word or words? The first letter of the required word is given.

1. He is a **very heavy** person. **C**
2. The position was obtained through **deceitful** means. **F**
3. He was reprimanded for his **rude and bold** language. **I**
4. The teacher gave me a **poisonous** look when I misbehaved in the presence of the school visitors. **V**
5. We found them to be a **cruel and harsh** people. **T**
6. My brother was, because of insufficient sleep, in a **drowsy** state during the performance. **S**
7. He comes from a **very wealthy** family. **O**

Word Origins

DAYS OF THE WEEK

Sunday

The first day of the week has been called after our most important planet, the sun. It comes from the Latin **solis dies,** which means "the day of the sun."

Monday

Another important planet is the moon. The ancients thought it would be proper to name the second day of the week in its honor. The Latin is **lunae dies,** "the day of the moon." Thus, their **Moonday** is our **Monday.**

Tuesday

Although the Romans named this day after Mars, their god of war, the Anglo-Saxons decided to dedicate it to their god of war, Tiw. So their **Tiwesday** is our **Tuesday.**

Wednesday

The Germanic tribes that subjugated the Romans replaced the name of Mercury, in whose honor the latter called the fourth day, to that of their own god, Woden. In time, **Woden's day** became **Wednesday.**

Thursday

The same tribe decreed that their god of thunder, **Thor,** should also be honored with a day in his name. Hence, their **Thor's day** has become our **Thursday.**

Friday

Perhaps to escape the charge of being too partial to the gods, the conquering tribe assigned the name of the Germanic goddess Frigga to the sixth day of the week. **Frigga's day** or **Friday** has survived the centuries.

Saturday

The invaders, probably to show that they had a tolerant spirit, agreed to retain for the last day of the week the name which had been of Roman origin. **Saturn's day,** which is our **Saturday,** dates back to the earliest times.

135

Clinching Test No. 16

I. Substitution Exercise

mystify	ponderous	peremptory
plausible	phlegmatic	invalidate

Substitute a word from the above list for the boldface word or expression in each sentence:

1. She was too **slow and easy-going** to qualify.
2. The youngster's good work in school seemed to **puzzle** his parents.
3. It was an **apparently reasonable** plan that he submitted.
4. His not living up to the terms of the contract will **break** it.
5. That wrestler is a man of **very great** weight.
6. The letter to the employees contained many **positive** terms.

II. Pronunciation Exercise

Explain the meaning and pronunciation difficulty of each boldface word:

1. The writer gave an **epitome** of his latest play.
2. The old man attributed his **longevity** to moderation in eating and drinking.
3. The appearance of the police put a **quietus** to the trouble.
4. The transaction was accomplished in a most **secretive** manner.
5. For him to contribute a large sum to this drive would be **incongruous** with his past contributions.
6. Her hat was **pyramidal** in shape.

[169]

136

Vocabulary

Multiple-Choice Exercise

In the following sentences, the student is given the choice of three answers. He is to select the word or expression which best defines the boldface word. The dictionary should be consulted for the correct answers.

1. That is **authentic** which is (a) capable of being heard, (b) of a genuine nature, (c) pertinent to a manuscript.

2. Facetious remarks are (a) insulting, (b) humorous, (c) false.

3. An **equivocal** statement is one that (a) pertains to horses, (b) is false, (c) has two meanings.

4. To **derange** is to (a) put in order, (b) cook, (c) throw into confusion.

5. A **derelict** is (a) a worthless person, (b) a widow, (c) an impostor.

6. You are **dogmatic** if you (a) have a kennel, (b) are positive in your manner, (c) are a skilled mechanic.

7. Remarks are **incoherent** if they are (a) not clearly connected, (b) loudly uttered, (c) of an angry nature.

8. A **contempiative** person is one who is (a) sad, (b) planning trouble, (c) is given to deep thought.

9. Nostalgia refers to (a) homesickness, (b) unpleasant odors, (c) a head cold.

10. Opinions are **concurrent** if they (a) agree, (b) refer to present-day happenings, (c) are hastily formed.

11. Regeneration means (a) a decline, (b) people born in the same period, (c) a complete reform.

12. Proclivity means (a) a sharp descent, (b) a tendency, (c) a falsehood.

13. A **presumptuous** person is one who is (a) backward, (b) wealthy, (c) too forward.

14. Solicitude is a synonym for (a) loneliness, (b) anxiety, (c) laziness.

15. To be **incapacitated** is to be (a) rendered unfit, (b) beheaded, (c) overfed.

137

Adjective Drill

Because of the important role that adjectives play in one's speaking and writing vocabularies, more than average attention has been given them throughout this book.

The student should familiarize himself with the definitions of the adjectives in the following list in order to be able to answer correctly without hesitation the questions in the succeeding lesson.

vapid	Dull; spiritless; without much life or flavor.
cursory	Hasty; superficial.
defunct	Dead; extinct.
profuse	Giving freely; abundant; lavish.
fatuous	Foolish; silly; stupid.
callous	Hard; unfeeling.
adamant	Firm; unyielding.
strenuous	Very active; vigorous; requiring energy.
animated	Full of life or spirit; vigorous; lively.
compatible	Consistent; capable of existing in harmony.
submissive	Yielding; obedient; humble.
acrimonious	Stinging; sharp or bitter.

Exercise

1. Make each adjective modify three nouns.
    a. defunct _____ _____ _____
    b. animated _____ _____ _____
2. Construct original sentences with:

fatuous hopes	compatible ideas
fatuous argument	compatible people
turgid stream	profuse growth
turgid mass	profuse praise

3. How does **callous** differ from **callus**?

138

Information Quiz

I

What adjective contained in the preceding lesson would you use:

1. To describe a bank that was forced to discontinue operating?
2. To describe a meeting that was full of action?
3. To describe a statement that was ridiculously false?
4. To describe a person who could not be moved to pity?
5. To describe a speech that lacked color and feeling?
6. To describe decorations that are numerous?
7. To describe an editorial that is very sharp?
8. To describe opposition that is difficult to overcome?
9. To describe a people that acts slavishly?
10. To describe a survey that is superficial?
11. To describe a judge who adheres firmly to his opinions.
12. To describe colors that blend?

II. Exercise

1. Write an original sentence containing:

   a. The noun form of **animated**.
   b. An antonym of **compatible**.
   c. The verb form of **submissive**.
   d. The adverbial form of **profuse**.

2. Fill each blank with a noun form of one of the adjectives in the above list.

   a. The students displayed no _____ at the football game.
   b. The speaker alluded to the lack of _____ of the two factions.
   c. There is a _____ of roses in his garden.
   d. The people in the satellite countries were held in _____ for years.

Pronunciation

Note the definitions as well as the correct pronunciations for the following words:

1. grimace — A facial contortion; an ugly smile.
2. attaché — A member of an ambassador's or minister's staff.
3. piquant — Pleasantly tart; stimulating to the mind or taste.
4. satiate — To fill to excess.
5. requital — Repayment; return.
6. arraigned — Brought before a court for trial; accused.
7. sobriquet — A nickname.
8. raconteur — A person who is clever in telling stories.
9. preferable — More desirable.
10. comparable — Able to be compared.

Phonetic Forms

1. grimace — gruh mace', not grim'mus
2. attaché — at uh shay', not a tash'ee
3. piquant — pe'kunt, not pe'qunt
4. satiate — say'she ate, not sat'e ate
5. requital — re qye'tul, not re quit'ul
6. arraigned — uh rained', not uh ranged'
7. sobriquet — so'bruh kay, not soo bruh ket'
8. raconteur — rak on ter', not ruh kon'ter
9. preferable — pref'er uh b'l, not pruh fer'a b'l
10. comparable — kom'puh ruh b'l, not kom pair'uh b'l

Completion Exercise

Fill each blank with a word from the preceding list to complete the sentence:

1. With him loafing was _____ to work.
2. A real student can never _____ his thirst for knowledge.
3. He was _____ before the court for manslaughter.

4. The _____ told many humorous and appropriate stories.

5. The child's _____ after tasting a lemon evoked laughter from those present.

6. What _____ can we make for his many kind acts?

7. The pudding contained a _____ sauce.

140

Vocabulary

MULTIPLE USES

The average person fetters himself to a single use of a word. He employs it in the same type of sentence; to him, it has only one meaning. A study of the word **vital** will reveal the multiplicity of ways in which the adjective and its related forms or family members may be used. If the reader will bear this flexibility of meanings in mind in his future vocabulary work, he will find the results most interesting and profitable.

Vital

"(1) Pertaining to life; (2) essential to life; (3) basic; (4) fatal or serious; (5) having to do with data about births, deaths, etc.; (6) affecting the truth of something."

State the number (or numbers) of the definition used in each of the following sentences:

1. The heart is a **vital** organ.

2. Eating and sleeping are **vital** functions.

3. What he said was of **vital** importance.

4. The soldier received a **vital** wound.

5. Mr. Brown is now in charge of the **vital** statistics department.

6. Her refusal of the position proved to be a **vital** mistake.

7. The numerous strikes have dealt a **vital** blow to industry.

8. The question of giving assistance to the impoverished people of the world is a **vital** one.

Vitally (*the adverbial form*)

1. We are **vitally** interested in your undertaking.
2. Every country was **vitally** affected by the war.

Vitalize
"To give life to; to impart energy or vigor to; to animate."

1. The thought of an early victory **vitalized** the troops.
2. The speaker **vitalized** his talk with humor.

Devitalize
"To weaken; to render lifeless."

1. The intense heat **devitalized** the workers.
2. Too much exercise is **devitalizing**.

Vitality
"Strength; energy; liveliness."

1. Her long illness sapped her of her **vitality**.
2. His voice has lost its former **vitality**.

Exercise
Construct original sentences with:

    a. defamatory statement   **c. amplification** of sound
    b. harmonious atmosphere   **d. intensity** of effort

141

Vocabulary—Pedestrian English

Recasting Exercise

erupt	To burst forth.
heinous	Hateful; giving great offense.
impeccable	Free from error; faultless.
cumbrous	Burdensome; unwieldy.
diversify	To give variety to; to vary.
benignant	Kind; gracious.

[175]

| tantamount | Equal to. |
| contributory | Helping to bring about. |

fraudulent	Dishonest; obtained by unfair methods.
fragmentary	Incomplete; disconnected.
intermittent	Coming and going at intervals; periodic.
demonstrative	Showing one's feelings clearly.

Rewrite the following sentences, using words from the preceding list that will convey the original meaning:

1. His reputation was without a flaw.
2. If you mention that incident, he will blow up.
3. We received only bits of the report.
4. The load he was carrying almost knocked him out.
5. To win the nomination for office in that city is just as good as being elected.
6. There was a kind expression on the old lady's face.
7. The students threw their hats and coats into the air when their team won.
8. Why doesn't our professor switch to some other way of teaching this subject?
9. The pain seemed to come and go.
10. His laziness in school was a cause of his having to repeat the year.
11. That check is n.g.
12. He should be punished for that frightful crime.

142

Achievement-Test Words

Study the definitions of the following words preparatory to answering the questions at the end of the lesson.

1. savant	A man of learning.
2. austere	Harsh; stern; forbidding.
3. tenuous	Slender; thin.
4. anterior	Front; occurring earlier.

5. mediocre	Ordinary; average.
6. audacious	Bold; daring.
7. desecrate	To treat without respect.
8. recumbent	Lying down; reclining; inactive.
9. loquacious	Talkative; inclined to talk too much.
10. philanderer	A flirt.
11. inscrutable	Not understood; incomprehensible.
12. sophisticate	A worldly-wise person.
13. presentiment	A feeling that something will happen.
14. hypochondriac	A person suffering from imaginary ailments.
15. insurrection	A revolt; a rebellion.
16. lackadaisical	Listless; dreamy.

Cautions

1. In **savant** the letter t may or may not be sounded. The last syllable is accented.

2. The third syllable **dai** in **lackadaisical** receives the primary accent and is pronounced **day**.

3. **Tenuous** is in no way associated with the **tenere** family which denotes **holding**, for example, **tenacious**, **tenable**, and **tenet**.

4. Be sure to give four syllables to **presentiment**. Do not overlook the **i**.

5. Note the spelling of the last syllable in **mediocre**. There is not the choice that exists in such words as **theater, center, and caliber**.

Quiz

What word from the preceding list would you use:

1. To describe a fearless individual?
2. For a person who is always worrying about his health?
3. To indicate one who is well versed in literature?
4. For a young man who presumes that he knows all the answers?
5. To describe the wisdom of God?
6. To describe laws that are very severe?
7. To substitute for "a vague sense of approaching misfortune"?

[177]

8. In reference to a person who talks too much?
9. To describe a boy who never cares to do any work?
10. For the part that contains the head and gills of a fish?
11. To describe the position of a cat that is lying down?
12. To indicate that a person is a flirt?

143

Word Origins

saunter

This word derives from the pace of the medieval pilgrims who journeyed so many miles to the Holy Land. **Saunter,** a telescoped word, is derived from the French, **sainte,** "holy," and **terre,** "land." What was originally **sainte terre** has been compressed in English to **saunter.**

scrupulous

Have you ever gone bathing where you had to walk over many pebbles before you reached the water's edge? Did you run over them? Probably not, unless the skin on the soles of your feet was of leather composition. You picked your steps slowly and cautiously. **Scrupulous** comes to us from the Latin **scrupulus,** which means "little sharp stone." Thus is derived our English meaning of "very careful and cautious" for the word **scrupulous.** A **scrupulous** person is "extremely careful, particular, and exact" and adheres to what his conscience tells him is right and proper.

cynic

Cynic is derived from a Greek word which means "dog." The name was given to a school of philosophers who taught that enjoyment of every description should be despised. The members lived frugally as ascetics, denying themselves material pleasures. They were contemptuously referred to as "dogs" or as leading a dog's life. Later the term acquired the meaning of "contempt for the opinion of others." Today a **cynic** is looked upon as one who is a chronic complainer, and that is the precise modern definition of **cynical**.

supercilious

If you are haughty or arrogant, the term **supercilious** might rightly be applied to you. Why? Because it may be construed as "expressing your haughtiness by the position of your eyebrows." The word is derived from the Latin **super,** "above," and **cilium,** "eyebrow." Have you not seen a person whose facial expression registered disdain and scorn by the uplifting of his eyebrows?

144

Clinching Test No. 17

Completion Exercise I

vital	defunct	cursory	scrupulous
defame	fatuous	arraigned	fragmentary
austere	authentic	submissive	intermittent

Fill each blank with a word from the above list to complete the meaning of the sentence:

1. His answers were of a _____ nature.
2. Mary is very _____ about her homework.
3. The youngster was reprimanded by his parents for his _____ remarks.
4. The signature was declared to be _____.
5. Sleep and wholesome food are _____ to good health.
6. The newspapers have received only a _____ report of the disaster.
7. Latin is often referred to as a _____ language.
8. A hermit leads an _____ life.
9. There was an _____ ringing of the telephone throughout the meeting.
10. Lincoln's enemies failed in their attempt to _____ him.

11. It is believed that he will be _____ on the charge of treason.

12. The people in the conquered countries were very _____.

Completion Exercise II

Complete each sentence with the appropriate word or words.

1. A **fraudulent** act is one that is _____.
2. **Arrogant** persons are usually unpopular because they are _____.
3. A **derelict** is an _____.
4. An **adamant** judge is one who _____.
5. **Savant** is another term for _____.
6. A **cynic** is one who _____.
7. A sauce is **piquant** if it is _____.
8. An audience is **demonstrative** when it _____.
9. A **tenuous** argument is one that _____.

145

Some Spelling Rules

What trouble the spelling of little words can give us! At some time or other practically everyone has found himself in the state of doubt as to whether or not he should double the last letter of a word before a suffix. Do not worry if you have been and are still in that state of doubt, because it will be an easy matter for you to free yourself from it if you will study each rule that is presented.

The vowels are: **a, e, i, o, u.** All other letters are consonants.

Rule I. If a word of one syllable ends in a single consonant, and a single vowel precedes it, you should double the last letter or consonant before an ending or suffix that begins with a vowel.

Example: Take the word **plan.** It ends in the single consonant **n,** which is preceded by the single vowel **a.** Therefore, you will double the **n** before an ending that begins with a vowel:

plan	planning	planned
rob	robbing	robbed
din	dinning	dinned

Now study the words:

plane	planing	planed
robe	robing	robed
dine	dining	dined

Why is there no doubling of the letter **n** in **planing**? Because **plane** does not end in a single consonant but in a single vowel. The following suggestion may help clarify the rule.

If you drop a letter, you may not add a letter. Thus, in the word **plane** the **e** is dropped. Hence, an extra **n** may not be added.

Rule II. If a word of more than one syllable ends in a single consonant which is preceded by a single vowel, and **the last syllable of the word is accented,** then the last letter or consonant is doubled before a suffix that begins with a vowel.

Example:

omit	omitting	omitted

The word **omit** ends in the single consonant **t** which is preceded by the single vowel **i**, and **the accent is on the last syllable.**

Now examine the word **offer:**

offer	offering	offered

Why is the **r** not doubled? Because the accent is not on the last syllable.

Another word that is frequently misspelled is **benefit:**

benefit	benefiting	benefited

The **t** is not doubled before a vowel ending because **benefit** is accented on the first syllable and **not on the last syllable.**

refer	referred	reference

If the **r** is doubled in **referred,** why is it not doubled in **reference?** The reason is that **referred** is accented on the last syllable, whereas in **reference** the accent drops back to the first syllable.

Exercise

Select the proper word in the parentheses to complete the meaning of the sentence:

1. The injured football player was (hoping, hopping) across the sidelines.

2. The carpenter is (planing, planning) the surface of my old desk.

3. The doctor is (offering, offerring) his services to this worthy cause.

4. Many cities (benefited, benefitted) by the new legislation.

5. The athlete's ankle was (taped, tapped) by the coach.

6. There was a (dining, dinning) noise in my ear throughout the night.

7. We (defered, deferred) action on that measure until next month.

8. The (inference, inferrence) was that he would soon resign.

9. We hope there will not be another (occurence, occurrence) of the trouble.

10. The people in that community are very (clanish, clannish).

146

Words Having "Ie" and "Ei"

The difficulty involved in the spelling of the ie and ei words will be reduced to a minimum if the following facts are noted:

1. The rule applies when the diphthong or digraph, that is, the two letters ie or ei used to represent a single sound, has the sound of e as in me. Then the letter i comes before the letter e in the spelling of that word (relieve, grieve).

2. If the letter c comes before the digraph or two letters, then e will precede i (receive, deceit).

3. If the pair of letters has the sound of a, as in day, then e comes before i (weight, neighbor).

[182]

A few illustrations will clarify the above three points:

a. In the word **grief**, the **ie-ei** rule is in effect because the digraph has the sound of **e**. Therefore, **i** should come before **e**.

b. In the word **ceiling**, the digraph has the sound of **e** but it follows the letter **c**. Therefore, the letter **e** should precede the letter **i**.

c. In the word **weigh**, the digraph has the sound of **a**. Therefore, the letter **e** should precede the letter **i**.

Note that each of the following words follows the **ie-ei** rule:

siege	sleigh	shield
belief	perceive	deceiving

Exercise

Fill each blank with the proper word:

1. In the word **besiege**, the letter **i** should come before the letter **e** because the digraph has the sound of _____ and does not follow the letter _____.

2. In the word **conceit**, the letter **e** comes before the letter **i** because the digraph has the sound of _____ and comes after the letter _____.

3. In the word **reign**, the letter **e** precedes the letter **i** because the digraph has the sound of _____.

4. Such words as **forfeit, foreign,** and **sufficient** do not belong to or follow the **ie-ei** rule because the digraph has not the sound of _____ or _____.

5a. **Leisure** and **neither**, when pronounced **lee′zhur** and **nee′ther**, are exceptions to the **ie-ei** rule because the digraph has the sound of _____ but the letter _____ does not precede the letter _____ according to the rule.

b. **Leisure** and **neither**, when pronounced **lezh′ur** and **nye′ther**, do not belong to the **ie-ei** rule because the digraph has not the sound of _____ or _____.

c. **Weird** and **seize** are one-hundred-per-cent exceptions to the rule because they have only **one** pronunciation, the digraph has the sound of _____, the digraph does not follow the letter _____, and the letter _____ does not precede the letter _____ according to the rule.

[183]

6. The three words in the following list which do not belong to the **ie-ei** rule are _____, _____, and _____.

chief	freight	efficient
skein	achieve	sovereign
niece	relieve	counterfeit

147

Diacritical Marks

Why are the meanings of the diacritical or pronunciation marks in the dictionary, which can be thoroughly grasped in a comparatively short time, known to such a small segment of mankind? The answer is obvious. The schools and colleges have failed to present this important phase of vocabulary building in a vital and meaningful way. In the majority of cases, the pupils and students have been and are being left to devise a method of their own for discriminating between the various sounds. A procedure that has proved effective in high school and college classes is the following.

The student should:

1. Learn the names of the important symbols.
2. Know the sounds they represent.
3. **Have a guide word or key word for each symbol or mark.**

(The third suggestion or requisite is of extreme importance.)

I

Mark	*Name*	*Illustration*
ā	Long or Macron	tāble
ă̇	Half-long	fă tal'i ty
ă	Short or Breve	măt
â	Circumflex	râre
ȧ	Intermediate	ȧsk

1. The Long Mark. A vowel is long if it has a horizontal line over it. Such a vowel will be pronounced the same as it is sounded in the alphabet: ā ē ī ō ū.

Examples: māke, ēve, nīce, mōtive, dūke.

2. The Half-long Mark. A vowel is half-long if it has over it a horizontal line and a small line perpendicular to it. The vowel will be sounded similarly to the long vowel but with less emphasis or time. Usually it is found in an unaccented syllable: ȧ ė ï ȯ ü.

Examples: vȧ ca'tion, ė ro'sion.

3. The Short Vowel. A vowel is short if it has a crescent or arc over it, as: ă ĕ ĭ ŏ ŭ. For a guide word, you need only put a consonant before the vowel and the letter **d** after the vowel.

Examples: băd, bĕd, bĭd, sŏd, bŭd.

Some may prefer **t**-ending guide words, as: **cat, get, hit, got, cut.** (The student should have only one key word for each symbol.)

4. The Circumflex. This mark is found only in the vowels â, ô, û. The letter **r** usually follows the circumflexed vowel.

Examples: **bâre, bôrn, bûrn.**

5. The Broad A. It contains two dots over the ä. An easy key word is **ärm.**

6. The Long U. For the sound of the long **u,** the student should pronounce it as though the letter **i** preceded it.

Examples: **tube** (tūb) Pronounce it **tiub.**

    tune (tūn) Pronounce it **tiune.**

7. The du and tu. When two letters are joined by a loop, as, dū or tū, the sound of the **d** or **t** is not pronounced as it is in the alphabet, but is blended with the following vowel.

Examples:

Word	*Diacritical Form*	*Pronunciation*
verdure	vûr'dūr	vur'joor
picture	pĭk'tūr	pik'choor
nature	nā'tūr	nā'choor

In order to understand thoroughly the diacritical marks, the following drill or procedure is suggested. The student should write the phonetic form of the word and state his key word for each marked vowel.

Examples:

Word	Phonetic Form	Key Words
active	ăk′tĭv	a as in **cat**, i as in **hit**
taste	tāst	a as in the alphabet
carefree	kâr′frē	a as in **care**; e as in the alphabet
hallway	hôl′wā	o as in **born**; a as in the alphabet

Exercise

In the column at the left are the pronunciation or phonetic forms of words. In the second column the student should write the required words. In the third column he should write the key word that he associates with each vowel. Too much emphasis cannot be placed upon the importance of having a key word for each symbol.

Phonetic Form	Word	Key
1. ē mûrj′	emerge	e as in the alphabet; u in **burn**
2. dē′pō	————	—————————————
3. twī′līt	————	—————————————
4. ăd hēr′	————	—————————————
5. tär pô′lĭn	————	—————————————
6. rēd	————	—————————————
7. bāt	————	—————————————
8. gāj	————	—————————————
9. nū′nĕs	————	—————————————
10. vĕn′tŭr	————	—————————————
11. wô′tēr fôl	————	—————————————
12. sēl′ĭng	————	—————————————
13. yēst	————	—————————————
14. dĕ frôd	————	—————————————
15. vū′lĕs	————	—————————————
16. wā′sīd	————	—————————————
17. tōō′-fāst′	————	—————————————

148

Figurative English

Metaphoric or figurative English is a significant characteristic of American literature. That its use, when appropriately applied, enhances the style of both writer and speaker is a cogent reason for emphasis being placed upon it in our schools and colleges. The instructor should endeavor to show the relative ease with which this art may be acquired and should encourage the student to strive diligently to cultivate it. He should also stress the fact that figurative language should be spontaneous, natural, and not forced.

The two most important and most frequently used figures of speech are the simile and the metaphor.

A **simile** is a definitely expressed comparison, as, "The halfback ran like a deer on the football field." The comparison between the halfback and the deer is definitely expressed.

A **metaphor** is an implied comparison or a simile that is condensed in a single word, as, "The halfback was a deer on the football field." In this illustration, the swiftness of a deer is attributed to the football player, the comparison being implied. The metaphoric word is **deer**.

Other metaphoric examples:

1. The father gave the child a **blistering** look because of his flippant remark.
2. Professor Brown is a **pillar** of that college.
3. The speaker **fired** many abusive epithets at the administration.
4. Troubles have **cascaded** upon that country.

The above boldface words give the metaphoric touch to each sentence because of what they imply.

In the first sentence, the characteristics of boiling water are ascribed to the father's looks. The implication in the second sentence is that the support and security furnished to the college by Professor Brown is as the strength and firmness given to a structure by strong pillars. In sentences three and four, the student no doubt will see an implied comparison to a gun and to a series of small waterfalls.

[187]

Suggestions for Metaphoric Writing

Select the important word and ascertain what are some of its characteristics. Take the simple words **dig** and **fetter**. **Dig** means "to turn up the soil with a spade." "He will **dig** a trench" is the literal use of the verb. "We shall **dig** more deeply into the study of words" is the figurative use of the verb.

Fetter means "to chain down or to shackle." "The hands and feet of the slave were **fettered**" is the literal use of **fetter**. "He is **fettered** to the belief that he has a malignant disease" is the figurative use.

Selection Exercise

Select the metaphoric word in each of the following sentences and explain the comparison implied:

1. His speech was tainted with sarcasm.
2. A shower of abuse descended upon him because of his dishonesty.
3. He has an animated pen.
4. She liked to stroll through her garden of words.
5. Attorney Brown lacerated the defendant's testimony.
6. We should sympathize with him because of his gnarled disposition.
7. Their hopes for an early victory are beginning to falter.
8. Sometimes words lay dormant through lack of use.
9. He drank from the fount of sound judgment.
10. Her latest book hoisted her into prominence.
11. That family is immersed in grief.
12. Students should strive to garner a worthwhile vocabulary.
13. Never try to stifle another person's ambition.
14. Industries were prostrate during that period.
15. Sorrow transfixed his heart.
16. In a few years she spiraled down to disgrace.
17. He caressed the thought of some day being president of the bank.

Exercise

Construct original metaphoric sentences with the following words.

deluged	wounded	elevated	incisive
pierced	pulverize	wilted	tinctured

150

Figurative Expressions

The student should be able to explain the metaphoric sentences found in this lesson and then should write original sentences which will contain the expressions given.

tide of discontent
tide of prosperity

A **tide of discontent** was beginning to engulf the working class.

The **tide of prosperity** is now moving over our country.

Use in sentences: **tide of remorse; tide of hatred.**

bond of friendship
bond of suffering

This legislation will strengthen the **bond of friendship** between the two nations.

The two families seemed to be held closely together by a common **bond of suffering.**

Use in sentences: **bond of sympathy; bond of helpfulness.**

shower of praise
shower of condemnation

He received a **shower of praise** from the banquet speakers for his many achievements in medicine.

Mr. X could not escape the **shower of condemnation** that followed his speech.

The verb:

They **showered** the hero with gifts and money.

Use in sentences: **shower of sympathy; shower of abuse.**

buried in ignominy
buried in oblivion

The traitor's name is **buried in ignominy.**
The records of those men are **buried in oblivion.**

Use in sentences: **buried in silence; buried in defeat**

blaze of glory
blaze of publicity

He finished the baseball season in a **blaze of glory.**
She could not avoid the **blaze of publicity.**

The verb:

For years his name **blazed** throughout the world.

Use in sentences: **blaze of wrath; blaze of fury.**

harvest of success
harvest of souls

He reaped a **harvest of success** as a result of his diligence
and perseverance.
The missionary working with a benighted people brought to
God a **harvest of souls.**

Use in sentences: **harvest of regrets; harvest of hopes.**

The verb:

They are now **harvesting** the rewards of their experiments.

nursed in idleness
nursed in crime

That man was **nursed in idleness** throughout his life.
The electric chair was the end of Smith, who had been
nursed in crime.

Use in sentences: **nursed in optimism; nursed in tyranny.**

yoke of oppression
yoke of tradition

Attempts to free themselves from the **yoke of oppression**
proved futile.

We should strive to extricate ourselves from the **yoke of tradition.**

Use in sentences: **yoke of authority; yoke of taxation.**

legacy of debts
legacy of happy thoughts

That administration left us a **legacy of debts.**

Greater than wealth was the **legacy of happy thoughts** bequeathed us by father.

Use in sentences: **legacy of words; legacy of love.**

intoxicated with joy
intoxicated with power

The student was **intoxicated with joy** when he was informed that he had passed the examination.

The leaders became so **intoxicated with power** that they neglected their work.

taint of corruption
taint of bigotry

The **taint of corruption** was manifest in the transaction.

They could not efface the **taint of bigotry.**

Use in sentences: **taint of avarice; taint of bribery.**

The verb:

His mind was **tainted** by the reading of indecent literature.

Selection Exercise

Explain the meaning of each of the following sentences and select the word that is used figuratively. Construct original sentences containing the figurative words found in this exercise.

1. The act was smeared with graft.
2. The football team seemed to be inoculated with confidence.
3. The boy's hopes for a college education were punctured by his father's financial troubles.
4. His acceptance of the bribe tarnished his reputation.
5. The writer's thoughts were garbed in expressive English.
6. The student found himself engulfed in debt.
7. An atmosphere of sadness pervaded their home.
8. It was difficult for him to go against the tide of public opinion.

9. Mr. Smith embroidered his speech with many personal experiences.

10. A wave of prosperity has spread over the country.

11. The mayor followed unswervingly the path of duty.

12. Our casual meeting ripened into a real friendship.

13. Christianity is the cornerstone of a true democracy.

14. The spirit of determination glowed in his cheek.

15. His record was painted in the darkest of colors.

16. It was obvious that it was a watered report.

17. His pride was wounded because of his unsuccessful attempt to become governor.

18. The careless youth was easily caught in the web of villainy.

19. His expansive generosity was inscribed in the memory of his fellow citizens.

20. We have only scratched the surface of vocabulary building.

21. The teacher gave the insolent boy a withering look.

22. The mayor's efforts to improve the city were strangled by the lack of funds.

Index to Words

A

abate, 11, 152
abdomen, 108
aberration, 160
abeyance, 76
abhor, 108
abolish, 123
abolition, 124
abominable, 76
abstemious, 30
abstruse, 85
abundant, 20
accentuate, 32
acclimate, 28
accompanist, 79
accrue, 123
"acious" words, 166
acme, 78, 134
acquiesce, 69
acrimonious, 171
active, 156
acute, 135
adamant, 171
adequate, 85
adjacent, 152
admonish, 123
admonition, 124
adobe, 141
adroit, 59
adverse, 27, 31, 61, 90
advert, 27
advertisement, 108
affect, 58, 152
affirm, 123
aggrandize, 32
aggregate, 125
aggressive, 152
alarm, 62
alias, 16
alienate, 28, 140
aliment, 134
allay, 31, 61
allege, 31, 108

alleviate, 112
allude, 71
allure, 71
ally, 28
alternate, 108
alumnae, 15, 127
alumni, 15
amanuensis, 115
ambiguous, 30
ameliorate, 118
amicable, 30, 41
"ance" words, 167
anent, 134
anima, 106
animal, 106
animated, 61, 171
animation, 106
anniversary, 102
antedate, 5, 112
anterior, 176
anticipate, 84
antithesis, 126
apathy, 31, 117
append, 147
applicable, 165
appraise, 152
appreciative, 108
apprehend, 147
apprehensive, 31
approximate, 84
apricot, 108
aqueduct, 160
arbitrary, 60
archaic, 126
ardent, 85
arithmetic, 68
arraigned, 173
arrange, 156
arrogance, 47
ascetic, 126
askance, 78
aspect, 13
aspirant, 28
assail, 147

assertive, 84
assimilate, 57, 141
assuage, 131
assume, 147
astute, 147
asunder, 32
"ate" words, 140
athletic, 68
atrocious, 60
attaché, 173
attest, 75
audacious, 139, 177
audible, 43
auger, 154
augment, 84
augur, 154
austere, 176
authentic, 147, 170
autonomy, 17
autopsy, 2, 57
auxiliary, 41
available, 43
averse, 90
aversion, 27, 147
avert, 27, 108
aviation, 164
avidity, 56

B

ballot, 161
banal, 134
bathos, 134
bayou, 141
bedlam, 33
beguile, 117
belated, 43
beneficent, 71, 146
beneficial, 146
benevolent, 43
benignant, 80, 175
berate, 126
bereft, 32
bestial, 57

[199]